oh honey ...
i'm just getting started!

oh honey ...
i'm just getting started!

CONSCIOUSLY CREATE YOUR NEXT DECADE

Trish Walker

Published in the United States by
Life Catalyst Publishing LLC

ISBN: 978-0-9976358-0-5

Book cover design by: Michelle Rayner, Cosmic Design

Interior design by: Katie Mullaly, Faceted Press

To the person I used to be.

Without you I wouldn't be where I am today!

table of contents

foreword

I'm a gold miner. Not in the literal sense, with pickaxe and dynamite in hand, but metaphorically that is exactly what I do for a living. I spend a majority of my day searching for gold in the hearts and minds of people just like you and me. Who I am and my own life story isn't that important, because I'm simply the miner who found the gold that you are about to feast your eyes upon.

In my work I help people work through their most challenging issues and deepest wounds, finding gold in even the darkest places. I also help people turn their pain into their purpose, by taking all of their life's experiences and stories and aggregating them into a mission, a movement, or a book just like the one you are about to dive into.

I first met Trish Walker at a personal development conference that I was volunteering at as one of the coaches. We sat down at a high top table just outside of the conference room where I had 20 minutes to help her with her business and see if she would be a good fit for any of the coaching programs.

At first glance, Trish was different than many of the other people who I had sat down with that day. She was glowing, she was curious, and she had a look of awe in her eyes that one would usually see from a young child. Even before she opened her mouth I thought, *Cool. This woman feels different. I can't wait to see who she is.*

Within the first couple of minutes I was blown away by her story and everything that she had accomplished in that one life-altering year. After taking in all of the data, I reflected back to her that by capturing everything on her blog she had already written an amazing book that she could publish immediately to help others who are just like that earlier version of Trish who was scared to take the first step. I came up with a tagline that gave me goose bumps and said something to the likes of, "Everyone needs to hear this story."

We cried together as I told her this because people tend to cry when someone speaks life-altering truth. And as the words came out of my mouth, I knew and she knew that she was sitting on a gold mine.

The fact of the matter is, all of us are sitting on a gold mine, including you. Your stories, your struggles, your victories, your challenges, your pain, your pleasure, your accomplishments, and your failures are all gold when delivered to the right person at the right time.

I don't know what led you to pick up this book, but I have a hunch that it's because these stories are exactly the medicine you need and you are the right person in the right time to be receiving them.

All of us have something that we've always wanted to do, but few of us actually go out and do it. May this book be a huge permission slip from the Universe to go after whatever makes your heart sing.

Stay golden,

Michael Hrostoski

Author, Coach, and Founder of The School For Men

preface

"If my life was a book and I was the author, how would I want my story to go?"
    —AMY PURDY

The day before my fiftieth birthday in the year 2014, I got a text message from my eldest brother John. John is famous for thinking that my birthday is actually the day before it really is. He then chuckles and says he just wanted to be the first one to wish me a happy day. Although I appreciate it immensely, this year's message really struck a chord. It went something like this when he realized I would be turning the big 5-0: "Congratulations, you are now half dead!"

I paused for a minute and then responded, "Oh honey, I'm just getting started."

I approached my 50th with some trepidation. After all, 50 just seemed *so old.* My mom was diagnosed with Alzheimer's when she was all of 54. By her standard that meant I only had a few more quality years left. I am already suffering from CRSS, otherwise known as *Can't Remember Shit Syndrome.* Now here I was getting closer and closer to the supposed end-of-life, as I knew it. My family makes jokes when they want to relieve stress of Alzheimer's looming in the background, but I truly believe that underneath it all, when we each individually misplace something we secretly think, *Holy shit, I have it.*

After talking to a few other folks staring down middle age, especially women, I was really surprised to learn that society has brought us to a point at which there are differing opinions on reaching this particular milestone. Amongst my nearest and dearest, it seems *they* think 50 is pretty much a time to pack it in and pick out the coffin. Holy hell, let's write a new story, people.

When I turned 50 I was just beginning to take stock in where I was at this particular juncture in my life, and where I wanted to go from there. I was nowhere near ready to call it a day.

Having done the corporate gig, I'm now raising a creative, fun-loving 11-year-old son. I'm also turning my life around after dealing with a bad case of losing myself when I quit my corporate career. I am working on myself and am ready to seize my new decade in a big, bold way by starting a new career as a coach, speaker and author.

Getting back to my brother's comments the day before my birthday – his little joke sparked a personal revelation. When it comes to getting older, I don't have to do it the way society traditionally dictates. I can write a new story, especially one different from my mom's. I have the blessing of looking younger than I am. Combine that with adopting a child later in life who is just entering middle school, and I have been able to pretend I'm not entering my fifties.

Well, the jig is up. I'm no longer afraid to put it out there. In the past, I was afraid of what others thought of me, plus I had a bad case of *the-need-to-be-loved* syndrome. I was a people-pleaser who would do anything for anyone. Now, however, I'm proud of who I have become and who I am, regardless of what other people think.

While going through this healing process, I reached back into my family archives for examples of other strong women in my life. This brings to mind my beautiful maternal aunt who was like a surrogate mom to me after my own mom passed away. Aunt Dale, AKA Momma D, gave me one of life's greatest gifts. She sat with me for hours sharing the secrets of life as she had learned them. And then in her passing, she told me that she would come back as a monarch butterfly and let me know that she was still with me. To this day, my family and I see butterflies in the strangest places.

The reason I bring up Momma D is because she told me that her fifties were some of her best years, certainly better than her forties. She said her fifties gave her a good sense of who she was, and she learned how to use that sense to make herself happy. Case in point, later in life she spoke her mind and didn't give a shit what others thought. A lesson that I have learned from her, yet still need to implement more of in my own life.

While I pondered this new attitude, and turning 50, I came up with the idea of doing fifty new things in the year I turned 50. *This wouldn't be so hard*, I thought. I'm not talking about just going on trips or doing spa visits; I wanted this to be something more. I wanted to learn new things, visit new places and have *Aha!* moments.

I am here to tell you that all that plus more happened for me. I'm now 51, and doing fifty things the year I turned 50 was a catalyst for me to start a new business, give seminars, write books and blogs, and live each day with meaning, without being dragged down by other people's baggage or things.

In the pages that follow, I take you through one of the best years of my life. Not only was I not "half dead" once I turned 50, I came alive like never before. Thank you to my brother, John. You will never know how much you inspired me to live it up like never before. I love you, bro! Keep wishing me birthdays in your own "special" way.

introduction

Fifty! Holy Shit ... 50. It was a pivotal, huge year for me. People kept asking me how I felt about going into a new decade. You know what? It was great. Fifty kicks ass!! Now well ensconced in my fifties, I feel so much better than when I turned 40. Life is opening up in so many wonderful ways. I have garnered new information and knowledge that indicates this decade is going to be one of the best yet.

But when 50 was looming, I wasn't especially happy about embracing my new decade. To get over that, I decided to do fifty new things in the year I turned 50; kind of like completing a bucket list, except I didn't plan on dying any time soon after I was done. What *was* I trying to accomplish exactly by doing this? Even now, I'm not quite sure. I had so many ideas swirling around in my head at the time; attending race car school, getting scuba certified, and being a tourist in places I had never thought to explore, just to name a few.

However, I didn't want my 50 for Fifty list to be all about me and my pleasures. I also wanted to complete service missions, help others, and even try new things outside of my comfort zone. I wanted to walk away from that year feeling good about myself, and what I did to pay it forward!

Guess what? I did it.

Now I invite you to come with me on a 365-day journey of exploration. There were lots of changes, lots of forward motion, and certainly lots of fun. I've taken my experiences and turned them into what I hope are milestones for you to use as nuggets of wisdom to help you move into your new decades in a fashion that benefits you most.

Let the adventure begin ...

my first 50 for fifty
takes fear to new heights
CHAPTER 1

"By letting it go, it all gets done. The world is won by those who let it go. But when you try and try, the world is beyond the winning."
 - LAO TZU

It happened. I turned the great 5-0! What an amazing day in an even more fantastic week. I felt the love from folks that truly mattered. I had visits from cousins, gifts from family and friends, and lunch with some high-energy ladies. For the first time in my life, I arranged my own birthday lunch, so I guess that could be considered one of the first new things I tried immediately upon turning 50 (although technically I planned my party *before* I turned 50). I knew whom I wanted to invite, and it all shook out exactly as I desired. The love and light was very evident that day!

For my first official 50 for Fifty, I decided to conquer a long time fear. There was one particular hike that I'd always start, but never finish because of my raw terror of heights. It was the Stewart Falls trail in the Sundance Resort here in Utah. To start the hike, you take a chairlift up to a rim, then when you get off you cling to the mountainside because of a ten thousand foot shear drop down the *other* side – or at least it seems that way to me.

I had attempted this hike several times before, but always chickened out after I got off the chairlift and hiked in about half a mile. The absolute drop-offs on the side of the thin trail completely freak me out. I am not one who is good with heights. If we're driving on a mountain road without a guardrail, you can bet I'm in the backseat with a blanket over my head. It all comes down to my fear of being out of control. So in the case of Stewart Falls, I just couldn't do it.

But not *this* day!

This day I made a choice. Once at the top of the Stewart Falls Trail, I could take the chairlift down (as usual), OR I could ignore my fears and hike the rim. (*Hmmm... decisions, decisions...*) What made the difference this time is that I had my then ten-year-old son with me. The thought of him seeing his mom back out on this hike because of her fear of heights was no longer an option. I wanted to show him, and myself, that I could feel my fear and do it anyway.

So off we went.

As I hiked along the top, clutching any root or tree that prevented me from plummeting to my death, F-bombs flew through my mind. *Why the f#%k did I agree to do this? Whose f#%king idea was this? How the f#%k am I going to make it around the next bend without plummeting to the bottom of the earth?* Even though I couldn't escape these thoughts, I kept going anyway. This time I didn't let my fear stop me. I had the goal of getting to the meadow where the trail flattened out and the views were gorgeous. And I knew it was just a little further ahead.

Or so I was told.

Apparently the short distance to the meadow was actually a crock of shit. My hiking buddies, which consisted of my son and his dad, exaggerated (i.e. lied) as a friendly way of encouraging me to forge on.

Regardless, I completed the hike and the views were well worth the spine-tingling expedition. That part about the breathtaking scenery was true. Stewart Falls is absolutely stunning. The waterfall, combined with the foliage, is a view everyone should witness.

When I finished hiking the trail, I turned around, and soaked in that magnificent view one last time. I felt an amazing sense of accomplishment. I set out to conquer one of my biggest fears, and I totally did it. It made me feel so proud of myself that I was already starting to think of what I could accomplish next.

At the bottom of the chairlift, I kicked back on a rock and celebrated my accomplishment with some dark chocolate — made all the sweeter by watching other folks who had taken the "easy way." Boy, they sure don't know what they missed by going that route. In fact, I never knew what I'd missed, until now.

As I completed my first "new" thing for my new decade, it became apparent to me that I could do not only this, but 49 additional new things in the coming year. I can do it and I did. Hiking the Stewart Falls Trail gave me a sense of purpose and awakened in me all the possibilities of the new things that I can try in the first year of my fifties. What a perfect way to begin my 50 for Fifty journey.

I could hardly wait until my next adventure!

now it's your turn

Are there certain things in your life you would like to accomplish, but fear stops you? List those fears in a journal. After writing them down, sit and imagine how it might feel if you actually pushed through any one of those fears and did them anyway. Then imagine how you would feel if you let a year go by and you didn't work up the courage to do any of them.

Find yourself a Courage Buddy; a person who will hold your hand and keep you accountable; preferably someone who has the same fear as you, and would be willing to work through it with you. Imagine the feeling of joy and accomplishment you both will feel having achieved your goals. There is nothing better.

braces at my age? really?
CHAPTER 2

"Dear Past, thank you for all the life lessons you taught me. Dear Future, I am ready now."
  - P.A. WALKER

I am not quite sure if this qualifies as an adventure, but for my next quest I got braces after years of having my teeth bonded in front. I had a huge David Letterman-style gap in my top front teeth, which I have struggled with for years. To cover it up, I had it bonded. But in my heart I knew it was still there. I finally realized that it was time to take care of this annoyance, because I was tired of letting it bother me.

But can you imagine? I am 50 and will have braces for the very first time ever? I spent weeks before my appointment, staring at people who already had braces. Was I going to be the oldest person ever to walk around with them? Would it inhibit my speech anyway? What would the pain level be? All kinds of thoughts swirled around in my head before my big day.

In order to get braces, the existing bonding on my teeth had to be taken off, thus leaving me with my huge natural gap for all to see. Eww. I could not fathom what this would look like, after not seeing it for years. But I decided to go for it anyway. Enough with the cover-up!

I had been working through my layers of emotional baggage, and like the gap in my teeth I was ready for a true, permanent fix. Why? Because something triggered in me back in my 40s, and as a result I started to look within. I worked with therapists, coaches, went to several workshops and some retreats. I knew there was a better way to live and I searched to find it. As I progressed on this path, I felt increasingly comfortable about being my true self – starting with my appearance. I guess whipping out a huge hole in my teeth is a symbolic step.

On B-Day (Braces Day) I had an anxiety attack. Going into the appointment, I wasn't as brave as I thought I'd be. My ego got the best of me. I had no recollection of just how big my tooth gap really was. The voices in my head reminded me that walking around with this gaping hole in my smile would be embarrassing. Again, I went back to my good old *"what-will-people-think"* mentality. But this time I shook it off. I marched right up those stairs, burst into the orthodontist's office, and went boldly into the unknown.

Well, when the time came to take the bonding off, that damn gap was even more gargantuan than I remembered. I knew it was the size of the English Channel Chunnel when the dentist winced and exclaimed, "Lord all mighty, that is one huge hole!" It didn't help that his eyes were bulging with disbelief. I muttered something about how I should have done this years ago and he agreed without hesitation.

But in the end, pulling off the bonding was not a big deal, much to my relief. (Wow! Who knew?)

Now that the dentist was done, it was on to the next step.

As I laid in the comfy chair and waited for the orthodontist to come in to start the next phase of fun, I rubbed my teeth along the newly freed gap and thought to myself, *Why didn't my parents do something about this after that horrendous seventh grade picture – the one with my school uniform courtesy of Immaculate Heart of Mary – that awful school I was forced to attend?*

My mom pulled me out of public school in the seventh grade and put me in Catholic School. Yuck! Why? Did she think she was going to save me? Did I need to be saved? Apparently so, because I was the only one of five kids who had to endure this torture. Back in those days, I did not dare to express my true opinions on how going to Catholic School was not on my wish list. I had seen previously how my brothers were punished if they went up against my parents. I, myself, had been on the receiving end of the wooden spoon many a time. When it came to something this big, I still could not bring myself to argue.

This brought me back to the day when my mom said I was leaving public school in sixth grade and moving into seventh grade at the local

Catholic school. (*Wait, what?*) I wish my mom were still alive so I could ask her reasoning behind that. I just assumed it had to do with the fact that my three older brothers and sister ran her ragged with their antics. I guess she thought she could save me from one's typical teenage years.

But I didn't want to be saved.

I begged. I pleaded. But it did no good. So there I was in my polyester uniform on the first day of school, having no idea what was ahead. To this day, all I really remember about Catholic school is that I somehow survived. On the bright side, perhaps it had a hand in why I am the *different* one in the family. I'm the only one who seems to seek answers to certain questions, and then actually makes an effort to go out and look for them.

Sitting in that orthodontist's chair, remembering all this, I decided right then and there not to get caught up in the regrets and anger of the past. I realized that my path had me wait until this exact moment to go through this experience. It's taken me a long time to realize that I am here on earth for something bigger than what I was told when I was younger (that being the perfect female who grows up to be either a nurse, a teacher, or a stay-at-home wife and mother). I've come to this realization through hard work, and thankfully it's paying off. You just have to understand that if you don't make even the smallest of changes in your life, nothing will change.

I have always had this feeling that there's something more out there for me. What it was I really didn't know until I started to write this book. We are all here for some special reason. People will always ask that question, *"What is my purpose in life?"* Heck, even my 11-year-old has asked me that. I tell him the mere fact he questions is proof that he's here for his own big reason.

Sit still, meditate, and ask for the answer. It will become apparent. It might take 51 years, but it will become apparent when you are ready to listen.

Turns out, the actual application of braces was not bad at all. It only took maybe an hour. I relaxed into my yoga breathing and all was fine, except for the orthodontist's assistant who kept reminding me that she would rather be home than in here wrangling my expansive tooth gap.

(Doing what? What could be more fun than staring down at the enormous gap in my teeth? Imagining a better future for my mouth?) At the end of the procedure she worked up enough positive energy to tell me that she was excited to see how it all would turn out.

After I received a round of congratulations from the staff and my free Park City Orthodontics T-shirt, my sore mouth and I went to lunch for a friend's birthday. It was the usual giggle fest, which was just what I needed after my morning of big changes. The ladies reassured me that my gap didn't look all that big. Okay, I know they were lying, but still it was nice to hear. What are friends for, right?

In the end, fixing my tooth gap was the perfect way for me to open up my mouth and show the world that it's okay. I am okay with how I look right now with braces, because I know it will all work out how I want in the future. It is a powerful message to love each day and be patient, even when these are the days you didn't necessarily want to go through. I know I must wait. It will take a year for my tooth gap to close.

In the meantime, I will be renting myself out as a beer bottle opener at weddings.

This whole experience of permanently fixing the gap in my teeth shows me that I'm able to take charge of my life. It's pretty empowering to not just think that, but believe it. And I do. Although it took years to get here, literally starting when I put on that Catholic School uniform (and not feeling like I had a say in the matter) to sitting in that chair at the orthodontist's office. I've got this. I'm going forward to a new phase in my life. I have a voice and I am not afraid to use it.

now it's your turn

Where do you need to speak up in your life? Is it at work, in your family or to a friend? Take this opportunity to sit and practice saying what you need to say. Write it out in a letter. Sometimes it's even better for you to write that letter and then destroy it. The mere act of "putting it out there" may give you the courage to speak up the next time you really have something to say.

stuff can't fill the heart
CHAPTER 3

"To live fully, we must learn to use things and love people, and not love things and use people."
- *JOHN POWELL*

After unpacking loads of boxes during a remodel and a move, it became very apparent that I have way too much stuff. What do I need all this stuff for? How did this stuff get into my house? Why does my son need all his stuff and why do I need closets and boxes full of stuff? What kind of example am I setting for my son? My Aha moment was the fact that I woke up and realized that it is time to de-clutter, sort through and donate most of my worldly belongings and keep it to the bare minimum of the essentials that I need to operate in my world today.

After a family discussion, we decided that for my son's birthday this year, we would set up a donation page for one of our favorite charities, Reach Out Worldwide (*www.roww.org*). He surprisingly agreed and as a result, his friends (or at least his friends' moms) also thought this was a great idea and they jumped on board. My purpose in all of this was that my son would see that there were others in the world in need. Instead of him collecting presents from his friends, in order to add to his pile of "stuff," he would be able to have them donate money to this charity and he could see that it would help those in need.

As a result, my son raised over $100 in donations for this great charity. He was excited to watch the total grow and I heard him telling his friends how he chose to do this and what the charity does. I was overcome by that proud Momma moment, and glad to see that he hadn't tipped too far into the *"I-love-and-want-my-stuff"* direction! Not once did he focus on not getting new toys or gifts for his birthday. Instead he got a kick out of watching the promotional video on the Reach Out Worldwide website, so he could tell everyone where his raised donations would be put to use.

After seeing my son's selfless act, I decided that it was time for me to also give to others. To be honest, I have had it pretty darn good thus far in life. Honestly, I've never been in *need*. I have only ever *wanted* the things that I *thought I needed*, in order to satisfy some ideal that I believed to be important. For example, the American Dream – the house, the car, the 1.5 kids. Funny what society throws at us and tells us that we need to uphold.

The year I turned 50 was the first in which I developed a new way of living. Instead of worrying so much about what others thought, for the first time in my life, I only worried about what *I thought*. It's been hard and it's still a work in progress, but I'm gaining ground. It's been surprising how good it feels to give to others. I heard a quote once that really spoke to this way of living:

"When you put good will out there, it's amazing what can be accomplished."

– *Paul Walker, Reach Out Worldwide Founder*

In addition to founding Reach Out Worldwide, Paul Walker (no relation to me, by the way) was a notable actor who tragically died at the age of 40 in a car crash. Most known for his portrayal of Brian O'Connor in *The Fast and the Furious* movie franchise, Paul is a great example of someone who could have given into the charms of Hollywood fame and all its perks. But he instead chose to use his money and notoriety to help those in need. After his untimely death, other family members stepped in to uphold his legacy. Yet another example of putting others first.

My lesson in all of this is that the time for me has come to turn my life from one of just being and doing into one of looking out for my fellow human beings, as well as for myself. I keep going back to the notion that we are role models for our children. Simple as that!

now it's your turn

What is an *Aha!* moment that you've had recently? Did you act on it? If not, think about why not and what stopped you. Think about how your life might shift by acting on that moment!

In honor of Paul Walker and his charity, please consider donating to Reach Out Worldwide. For more information about this wonderful organization, please head over to www.roww.org.

life lessons
from the tubing park
CHAPTER 4

"There is no illusion greater than fear."
  - *Lao Tzu*

This adventure started out benignly enough. I had a Groupon for a snow tubing session at Soldier Hollow here in Utah. Soldier Hollow is the former site of quite a few cross-country ski events during the 2002 Winter Olympics. It's a gorgeous venue with scenery of mountains, blue skies, and a rather large tubing hill.

For those of you who live in warmer climates, let me explain what snow tubing is: it's defined as the sport of moving across snow on a large inflated inner tube. I define it as sticking my large derriere in a rubber thing and then whistling down a hill at top speeds on a combination of snow and ice while holding on for dear life.

After booking a session, I headed out to Soldier Hollow with my son, a friend, and her family. The evening weather was wonderfully warm (for a Utah winter, that is) and the sky was filled with many stars. We got into our tubes and headed up the rope tow towards what promised to be a night full of fun.

The first run was fantastic. All five of us swapped ropes and bonded together for a joint joyride down the hill. It was so fast and exhilarating that I just remember whooping it up and giggling the whole way. It was so cool!

The next run it was just me and my kid. However by then the temperature dropped and the course was super slick. Again, we screamed all the way down and *assumed* that we would stop at the bottom. However, the course had a different idea. In an instant, I realized we were going to crash through the snow fence. And sure enough… we did. Right before impact, I remember having all kinds of thoughts flying through my brain. How much will the doctor bills cost me, can I shield my child and sacrifice my body and I hope this isn't too painful. After we broke through a snow fence, I was relieved to find that both my body parts and my son's were still intact.

We both survived the scramble with nary a mark on either of us. However, it did set the tone for the rest of the night. I took in the fear element and my son, well, he thought it was a screaming good time. I had to remind him that crashing was not part of the price of admission.

I immediately shifted into an *even bigger* mental state of fear. Pure, raw fear. Each run had me so worried about the ending, that I stopped enjoying the rides down. But I put on a brave face and kept going because I would not let this stop my fun. Or at least my son's fun. It was not until the last run that my fear came true. This time I was all by myself, going so fast, that even when I dragged my feet on the ice, I completely sped right by the course operator at the bottom. I went through not one but two snow fences. I heard my glasses shatter (or something shatter), but after I finally skidded to a stop, I got up and realized both me and my glasses were still in one piece. I waved my glasses in the air and yelled, "Thank God for Costco!" My glasses took the blow from the pole. I escaped with some minor abrasions and lived to tell the tale.

Why am I telling you this story? After my run, I decided I'd had enough. I sat on the side and watched everyone else hoot and holler and thought to myself, *What a metaphor for life.* I was so focused and fearful of my ultimate end that I didn't enjoy the ride leading up to it. I realized that this evening of tubing mirrored my own life. What am I doing to enjoy the ride leading up to *my* ending? What can I do every day to enjoy the *ride*?

People worry so much about death, or how they are going to die, that they don't enjoy the day-to-day. Until I took this ride, I didn't even understand that I had become one of those people. If I fly somewhere, I think about what would happen if the plane dropped out of the sky. If I am on a highway, I think about the fatalities that could happen. I'm not sure what precipitated this kind of thinking, but I suspect it might be partially media-driven. I finally stopped watching the news, because it's so terrifying that you can't help but bring it into your everyday life.

If we spend too much time thinking about the end of the story, we don't enjoy the juicy chapters happening as we read the book. We can't appreciate life's little mysteries if we skip directly to the end. Heck, I even noticed I was doing it during a 60-minute massage. I would literally time my massage in my head so I wouldn't be disappointed when it was over. I couldn't just relax and enjoy the experience.

But I have since learned how to surrender. It took me seeing several loved ones die too soon, or worrying about things over which I had no control, before I could truly enjoy an experience. My tubing crashes certainly were the start of a new way of thinking for me. Imagine that, it all gets back to laughing, surrendering, and acting like my old childlike self.

I look back on that final run and realized that right before I knew what was going to happen, I just surrendered and let go. It probably saved me a few scratches by relaxing into it. Time to do that in real life!

Before I left the tubing park that night, I asked the course dude why he didn't stop me as I flew by. He simply replied, "Because you were going way too fast."

I agree. And that's why I've decided to slow down and enjoy the ride.

now it's your turn

Next time you suddenly feel afraid, just remember this great acronym: **FEAR = False Evidence Appearing Real!**

want-to-be writer
turned real writer
CHAPTER 5

"Incredible change happens in your life when you decide to take control of what you do have power over instead of craving control over what you don't."

- STEVE MARABOLI, LIFE, TRUTH AND BEING FREE

I have always been a voracious reader. I love to read books, magazines, and blogs, you name it. One day I decided to turn the tides and become a *want-to-be* writer. Why did I keep labeling myself a *want-to-be*? I AM a writer. I have published lots of blog posts on my personal blog *www.50forayear.com*. I have also submitted several articles for publication.

Now for one of my 50 for Fifty firsts, I decided to write not one, but two books. I have two distinct ideas for books and somehow they keep melding into each other. Should I combine or separate them? I'm just not sure. The whole point of my 50 for Fifty adventure was to surrender to ideas and see where the Universe takes me.

Before this book (the one you're reading right now) I wrote a previous book, and finished it to the point of a first-draft. I sent out word to two different people to help edit and got no response. Instead of giving up, I surrendered and moved on to the second book, which is the one you're reading at this moment. Obviously, I moved forward with this book, and have a plan in place for the *next book*.

Getting back to my first book, I thought going to an author's event might help me to figure out what to do about the editing. I felt like this is what I was supposed to do. Again, surrender to the Universe. Why is it so hard to surrender to the Universe? This question kept coming up whenever I tried to surrender, but then failed. Are you supposed to surrender completely or help the process along? And if you are supposed to help the process, what does *that* look like?

I think the reason I found it so hard to surrender is because I'm one of those folks who needs structure. If you come to visit me for a week, you get a schedule like you were staying on a cruise ship. When I go away on vacation, I need to know what I'm doing every single minute. This is not new for me. But now I see that if you just trust and let go, great things come to you. It's hard for someone (like me) who has moved a lot and had family tragedies, all of which contribute to control issues. How's that been working out? Not so well. I knew it was time to switch it up. Learning how to surrender works for me. So far, so good!

"I surrender this fear or desire. Thank you for taking care of it!"

now it's your turn

Take a little time here to stop and think about how a situation would look if you were to just surrender to it. Is there an area in your life in which you are holding on too tightly? How is this working for you? Can you take a new approach and re-frame it? Can you, for instance, treat someone you love differently? Stay in your own lane instead of offering your advice, which might be falling on deaf ears. If someone is not ready to hear something, it ends up being exhausting for both of you. Is there an area in your life where you are worrying about something so much that you exhaust yourself? Can you let it go? This is a great time to just sit, meditate, and throw it out to the wind!

not so fast
and not so furious
CHAPTER 6

"If everything seems under control, you're not going fast enough."
- *MARIO ANDRETTI*

I did it! I went to race car school. It's been on my bucket list for years now and I finally made it happen. After growing up in a family of boys, it was in my blood to like cars. One of my brothers owns a towing/salvage business and the other works for an auto auction company. My brother with the towing business logged in time hauling away some pretty fancy vehicles at IndyCar events. It wasn't unusual for me to share a ride in the truck with one of the Andretti's or some other famous race car drivers. It amazes me now that I didn't end up doing something in the race world as a career. It only made perfect sense that one of my 50 for Fifty items was to attend race car school.

When I finally went, I trained at Exotics Racing in Las Vegas. The staff was amazing and my experience was beyond awesome. I left the track that day saying that was one of the coolest things I'd ever done in my whole life. It truly made me feel really alive.

After sitting in a class learning about technique and going around the track once to get some instructions from a seasoned professional, someone actually handed me the keys and allowed me to get behind the wheel. For this adventure, I chose to go out in a Porsche Cayman. Although it was referred to by some of the drivers at Exotics as the "go-cart" of the racetrack, I was still thrilled to be able to get out there and make some turns.

My instructor hailed from the U.K. and was a very patient man. I swear he had nerves of steel. He instructed me all the way around the track five times. I slowed way down around the curves, but finally got up the gumption to turn up the speed towards the end of my session. When I reviewed the video of my laps, I burst out laughing because at each turn it looked like I was slowing down to get a parking spot at the mall. When I originally heard that I'd *only* get to do five laps, I thought to myself, *Well, that's not enough.* Turns out I was very wrong. It requires a lot of hard work and strength to do even *one* lap. Each trip around the track requires muscles I haven't used in a very long time. I have a whole new appreciation for the drivers who do an entire race!

As I left my vehicle, I felt like I still hadn't experienced the thrill of speed. I realized that I had let fear once again hold me back. Shoot! I regretted that I hadn't just let the car fly around the track. To satisfy my as-of-yet unmet need for speed, I decided it was time to take a few laps with a professional race car driver at the wheel (and me as the passenger).

My driver's name was Rudy and his credits included being one of the stunt drivers in the first *Fast and Furious* movie. I thought I would be completely nervous going into this adventure, but in fact, just the opposite was true. Once we started around the track I had such a feeling of calm come over me that Rudy could see I wasn't scared at all. I think he took this as a challenge and turned up the heat. During our last lap, we completely drifted and swung around. I still wasn't freaked out. Sorry Rudy, you can't scare this old gal! Afterward I made a vow to go back and do it all again very soon. Next time I plan to drive the Lamborghini.

After completing my racecar adventure, I left the track on such a high. From then on, I vowed I would not continue to hold back because of fear. I would put myself out there and feel the fear and do it anyway!

With each new adventure, it's amazing how I start to chip away at the fear that has held me back from living a full life. I look back and try to see where this fear started and why I held onto it for so long. I think it's a combination of family stories, life experiences, becoming a parent and not wanting my child to experience the loss of me. However, when I deeply look at it, there's nothing to fear but fear itself (thank you, Franklin D. Roosevelt).

As I now tell my child, roughly 95 percent of things you're scared of never come true anyway. Let's all live with that in mind.

<u>now it's your turn</u>

Where can you let go of some fear? Where did your fears originate and what will letting go of that "old story" buy you? I urge you to take a moment to think about this. Do you always say things like, "Oh, I would love to do that, but…" and then you never quite seem to get around to doing whatever "that" is?

Change your thinking. Make doing whatever it is you're afraid of a priority. If you can find that Courage Buddy (I mentioned earlier) to hold your hand, I say go for it. Just having the comfort of someone there with you might be the nudge you need. Go out and get some brochures for that sky diving course you've always wanted to take. Bungee jump off a bridge. Take a high wire trapeze class. Whatever it is, make it a goal by the end of the next week. Take that one item off of your *Would-like-to-do* list and move it to your *Now-I-can-post-cool-pictures-on-Facebook* list!

the circle of influence
CHAPTER 7

"The fellowship of true friends who can hear you out, share your joys, help carry your burdens, and correctly counsel you is priceless."
- EZRA TAFT BENSON

As I continue on with my new decade I have the feeling that no matter what I try to do to improve, my past keeps following me in an attempt to dictate my future. So far I'm able to resist, but it still persists.

Case in point, I have been working on "upgrading" my circle of influence. When I first heard that you're the sum total of the five people closest to you, I looked around and was aghast. These were not very confident or ambitious people. At that point I started to work on myself, because in that present state, I attracted people that didn't fit with my definition of success. I was around some folks who were not very uplifting. Did I do this because I wanted to feel better about myself, and being around uninspiring people accomplished that? Most likely the answer was yes.

After making this realization, I set about surrounding myself with some like-minded folks who could help elevate me to where I wanted to be. I went on retreats, took classes, and did a whole lot of reading. Then one day, I looked around and realized I had done just what I set out to do. I succeeded in surrounding myself with a great group of *new* people who not only are always there for me, but also uplift me. They *want* me to succeed.

When I made that decision to upgrade my circle, I researched ways of getting myself out there and meeting new people. I came upon a six-week online course called Six Weeks to Your Greatest Self (*www.jessebrisendine. com*). This led me to meeting some like-minded folks on Facebook, in my town and in the surrounding areas. I signed up for some weekend retreats within several hours of my home and this in turn helped me to make some life long friends. If you take one new avenue a week and go from there, I guarantee that you will look up one day and realize that you have been given the gift of changing up your circle.

So what's the problem?

The problem is that my past keeps giving me pop quizzes. People appear out of nowhere to test how far I have really come. For example, after spending yet more of my precious time with a complaining friend who just doesn't want to look inside, I'd had enough. I blurted out, "If you don't change, then why do you think anything around is going to change?" I asked. My friend looked at me like I'd just had a small seizure and then uttered those words that I forbid myself and my child to use: *"Yeah, but…."*

It was at that moment that I realized not only did I have the tools to work myself out of my own *"Yeah, but…"* situations, but that I was finally ready to actually use them. I looked at her and again said, but louder this time, "If you don't change anything, how do you expect your situation to ever change?" She continued to defend herself, but by then I'd really had enough. I got up, told her that I had to go, and then walked away.

This was a huge first for me. It might not have been the proper way to handle the situation, but I think she got the message. Why do I continue to go back into these toxic circumstances when I know they are not good for me?

It's fear. Simple fear of letting the other person know how I feel and fear of conflict. It comes down to the perpetual need to be loved and liked. It has taken me a long time to get to this point, but I know now that I have the tools to upgrade my circle of influence and I certainly will not hesitate to use them if needed.

In the meantime, I made a point to reach out to my newest "circle of influence" folks and let them know how much I appreciate each and every one of them. I'm grateful that they came into my life at just the right moment.

now it's your turn

Have you have ever been held captive by someone else's negativity? How did you handle it? Are there situations in your life in which you still need to "clean" house a bit?

I recently returned from a workshop where I heard this tasty bit of insight. You have three layers of people in your life.

The first layer includes your closest confidantes. You give them the real deal. You divulge things you wouldn't tell anyone else. You know you can trust them.

Layer two consists of those people you share maybe 50 percent of your life with. They are the folks you pass along ideas to, get feedback from, and share good times with.

Your acquaintances make up the last layer. These are the people you work with, neighbors, your kids' friends' parents, etc. You don't divulge too much personal information to the people in this group, because you just don't know them well enough to trust them.

Take some time to figure out your own circle of influence and how shifting some folks from one layer to another might put you in a better situation to live a less stressful life.

As for me, I know that shifting several people in my life to the outer limits of Layer Three has helped me immensely!

a four-day adventure
(to the tune of a three-hour tour!)
part 1
CHAPTER 8

"Traveling – it leaves you speechless, then turns you into a storyteller."

   - IBN BATTUTA

Continuing on with my 50 for Fifty adventures, I found myself being called to the beautiful Red Rocks of Sedona, Arizona. I've been here before, so the first for this particular adventure is the fact that I have never driven there from my home base of Park City, Utah. People told me I was crazy to drive ten hours by myself. But I was actually looking forward to slowing down and having more than a few hours alone in a car with nothing to do but pay attention to the road and listen to books on tape.

The first day out I drove six hours straight and spent the night in Kanab, Utah. I have never been in this part of my home state and was looking forward to seeing what it had to offer.

All the way from Park City to Kanab, I listened to the audio CD of the book, *The Secret* by Rhonda Byrne. *The Secret* started out as a documentary in which Ms. Byrne teaches us that we are the architects of our own lives, with every thought, in every minute, of every day. *The Secret* offers tools and ideas to help you live more fully, so that you are able to create the life of your dreams. I have seen the documentary, but for some reason on this particular drive all alone, the audiobook was really speaking to me. I enjoyed it so much I re-listened to it on the way back from Sedona, as well.

My first night in Kanab was a mixed blessing. On the one hand, it was nice to stop after being in the car for so long. I stayed at the Holiday Inn Express. If you've ever been to Kanab, you know this is the hottest hotel to stay in town. On the other hand, the walls of this Holiday Inn Express are so thin the adjacent screaming babies and barking dogs kept me up almost all night. I tried to let it go and get back to sleep, but after several hours of this non-stop noise, I was ready to swing open the door and invite everyone into my room for a party. After all, it wasn't like I was going to get any sleep anyway. I might as well enjoy the time spent for this room I had rented. It became almost comical. You know when you are in a hotel room and you feel like you are sitting on the toilet with the guy in the room next to you or having sex with the couple next door? This was how my night at the hotel went.

All was not lost though because the *real* blessing for me in Kanab was the Rocking V Cafe (*www.rockingvcafe.com*). This place has fabulous food and even better service. I had the SXSW Salad for dinner; a wonderful blend of black beans, toasted pumpkin seeds, jalapeño marinated chicken with cilantro lime dressing. I topped my fantastic meal off with a piece of key lime pie to go. My night in Kanab proved to be an ironic mix of both satisfying food and restless sleep. However, the road trip the next morning from Kanab to Sedona was beautiful and awe-inspiring in terms of scenery.

Stay tuned for the next installment in this first ever journey on the road from here to there!

now it's your turn

Where in your life can you go on an adventure? Is there a particular spot in your state where you keep saying that you have never been before and want to try out? Get that calendar out and make it a date. Be open to all the road has to offer to you. If I had let my first night on the road dictate the rest of my trip, I would have been in for a disappointing weekend. Instead, I took each turn as it came, and ended up having an amazing weekend.

second for sedona (part 2)
CHAPTER 9

"Travel makes one modest. You see what a tiny place you occupy in the world."

   - GUSTAVE FLAUBERT

The rest of my journey to Sedona was one filled with beautiful scenery, long empty roads, and lots of time to listen and absorb the CDs I had brought along. It's truly wondrous that there is still so much empty space left in our country. It re-energized me to see not one Target, Wal-Mart, McDonald's, or strip mall for miles. In fact, I didn't see one big box store all the way from Provo, Utah, to Sedona. I can't tell you what a great feeling this was.

Even though there was nothing for long stretches, I didn't once feel *alone*. I carried such a peaceful feeling with me throughout the drive. I trusted that someone or something was out there keeping an eye on me. If I had broken down in the middle of nowhere, not only was there no cell service, but it would've been a really long time before someone came along. Was I scared? No. Because I just totally trusted that I was okay. It has taken me a long time to be this peaceful in my own skin. It felt great and I was ready for a fun weekend in a beautiful place.

When you first pull into Sedona, you experience the most amazing scenery right from the get-go. The red rock formations are like nothing I have ever witnessed; beautiful hues of color. During my weekend there, I was treated to plenty of eye candy in the form of nature.

I also had the best meals at several restaurants, especially the Heartline Café (*www.heartlinecafe.com*). Definitely check out this restaurant. They have the most delicious French Toast stuffed with a delightfully light lemon crème. The food at the Heartline Cafe was so good that I ate there twice.

My second time going to the restaurant, I got talking to the owner of the restaurant. Phyllis and her husband have run their place for 20-plus years. I bonded with this woman immediately, and to make things even more special, we both realized that we grew up in New Jersey. In fact, her husband and I are both from the same very small community in the town of Wayne. We shared stories of how we both migrated out west and had had culture shock when we first arrived. We also shared stories of the foods that we missed from the east coast. Where else can you get a great bagel or pizza than in New Jersey. What a small world. Before I left, Phyllis gave me the official cookbook from their restaurant. It was such a great place to eat and just hang out. If you ever make it to Sedona, the Heartline Café is not to be missed.

The next day I had the pleasure of hiking for six miles round trip in Boynton Canyon. Some would say that's too much. But the scenery was so breathtakingly beautiful that I couldn't help but feel I was blessed to be able to do this hike. My cousin, who resides in Arizona, joined me on this glorious outing. She was a rock star, as we journeyed deep into the woods. We saw beautiful red rocks, trees, and stunning vistas. The trail ran alongside the property for the Enchantment Resort. For me, it was a special place tucked back into the wilds of Sedona, away from the touristic main strip. It was nice to get away from it all.

After our great hike, my cousin and I treated ourselves to a lunch like no other at a healthy eatery called the Chocola Tree Restaurant (*www.chocolatree.com*). Their menu was a very eclectic mix of organic fare. I ended up ordering about four things just because they all sounded so good. I finished my meal off with a Pachimama latte, a delicious mix of ginger, cinnamon, and love.

My time in Sedona came to an end very quickly. Before I knew it, I had to get back into the driver's seat and head home. I chose to push through and drive ten hours straight back to Park City. This time I took a different route and went through the Vermillion Cliffs area, which is at the top of Arizona. More spectacular scenery! Unless you actually experience this part of the world, it is very hard to put into words.

The last hour of my trip I struggled up Provo Canyon in a snowstorm. Snow. Ugh. I just left 75-degree weather and sun. I was tempted to turn right around and go back to Sedona, but figured I had a few folks back at home who might not be happy with that decision.

now it's your turn

Take some time to journal on a trip that you have been meaning to take but keep putting off. It could even be as simple as a new restaurant in your town that you have always wanted to try but just never made the time. Going out into an unknown world, even if it is just down the block, is a great way to see new things, meet new folks and perhaps make a connection with someone from your hometown. Make a list of five things that you have always wanted to try but just never did. Make these happen within the next month. The sense of accomplishment that you feel after just doing even one will most likely propel you forward into completing the rest of your list.

today the world was
one big family
CHAPTER 10

"The bond that links your true family is not one of blood, but of respect and joy in each other's life."
- R. BACH

How does one even explain this new adventure? Fate, universal love, karma, not quite sure what it is called. Last April brought with it an amazing first for me. I have never had the opportunity to attend a Hollywood premier. On April 1st, no fooling, that all changed.

Let me back up by saying that about two weeks before I left for California, I was standing in my kitchen and the overwhelming feeling that I was about to go to Los Angeles overcame me. Why did this happen? Not quite sure. I just thought to myself, I am going to be going. I am really learning to trust my intuition, so I proceeded on with my day with the understanding that I would be taking yet another trip.

I happened to jump on Facebook that same night and messaged a friend of mine and told her that I was going to be going to Los Angeles. She reminded me that the World Premier for the latest installment in the *Fast and Furious* franchise would be taking place soon. It didn't really register with me because I had never seen any of these movies, but my friend is a huge fan. I just felt it in my bones. I told her that if it were meant to happen, tickets to the world premier of *Furious 7* would just manifest. Again, remember I was now an "authority" on living the Secret after listening to it for ten hours. Well, I am here to tell you that this stuff really works.

Fast forward two weeks, one frequent flier ticket later and a link that once it was clicked sent me into the world of "Congratulations, you now have a ticket to the World Premiere of *Furious 7*" on April 1st in Hollywood, California. It's a long story on how this all evolved. It's a story of synchronicities, like-minded people, and coincidences that I normally wouldn't have been open to prior in my life. As I am learning to trust the

Universe, different opportunities are actually coming to me, starting with this movie premier. The abbreviated story on how this all came together begins with how I began doing work with someone who had a connection to one of the stars of the franchise. Through him, I met a woman who later became a good friend. She is a big fan of the movies. She kept up to date on all things *Fast and Furious* and was the one who happened to be on her computer that fateful day and saw the link to click in order to win the grand prize of being at the premier. To this day we still laugh about how this all came to pass. A series of coincidences, spirit guides and just plain good luck!

The Big Day Arrives

The morning of April 1st, I boarded a plane with an overloaded carry-on bag containing three outfits. After all, what does one wear to a movie premiere? I also boarded the plane not having seen *Fast and Furious 2* through *6*. I had speedily watched the original *Fast and Furious* after learning I was going to be going to the premier. My friends and family suggested that I at least get to know the players.

My plane landed amongst the beautiful palm trees, people and sunshine.

Heading to my hotel in Hollywood, I realized that right at that moment the ceremony for Vin Diesel getting his star on the Walk of Fame was taking place. There were so many people that all I could see was the top of his beautiful shiny head.

That Night at the Premiere

When you see pictures from these Hollywood events, it all looks so glamorous. Don't get me wrong it really *was* glamorous. However, it was also an endurance event.

Let me outline my day and night.

We started standing in line at 2:00 p.m. We were told to stay there and then someone would tell us where to go so we could get our wristbands. Since we had no concept of time, we were afraid to do anything; leave to go pee, get a drink of water, anything. We did (*we* being myself and my good friend who I first contacted about my gut feeling of going to Los Angeles) start to really get to know the other occupants of our line. There was that nice young couple who had left their child with grandma. We also befriended a lovely young lady who had been an extra in the movie. She had driven all the way from Northern California by herself. She was totally a fan. To this day, Jessica has become a good friend. We now share a love of the movie and have both watched it numerous times.

As the day progressed, 2:00 turned into 3:00 and all the way to 5:30. At 5:30, we started moving. Yes, I thought to myself, I was finally going to get my precious wristband and then find the nearest restroom.

I guess the April Fool's joke was on me. They ushered us right out to the red carpet! The red carpet in this case, was actually a black and white carpet that resembled a road. There were very cool cars parked all around. We stood in this area for several hours as all the celebrities and beautiful people cycled through their interviews, waving, coming up to us fans and signing autographs and taking pictures. I have to say, everyone was really nice.

We finally got in to see the movie at 11:00 p.m., which was amazing. So amazing, in fact, that I went to see it again three days later. What a beautiful tribute at the end for the late Paul Walker.

Several things became very apparent to me during this daylong experience. One: the cast of this franchise are very close and love each other dearly. They also really care for their fans. Two: after experiencing this movie premiere I can honestly say I may never do that again (too much standing around!). However, the best thing about that night was that this movie brought together fans, celebrities, rap stars, producers, family members, etc., from all different races, cultures, and for one night, it felt like all was right with the world. All was right with the world for one brief evening, because we were one big, happy family. It was truly a feeling I loved and will carry with me throughout the future.

now it's your turn

Has there ever been an instance when you felt a gut instinct and you went with it? Did it produce great results? We are all born with intuitive abilities, however it's those of us that develop it who see real results. I would love for you to take some time over the next couple of days and see where and when your intuition might be trying to get your attention. Was there an instance in which you chose one thing, but had the feeling you should have chose another? Have you ever thought of someone only to have them call you that afternoon?

These are all instances of intuition.

There are many classes, workshops and books that can give you more meaning into developing your intuition. It's amazing the gifts that can come from using your intuition to its fullest!

the power of words

CHAPTER 11

"One of the most sincere forms of respect is actually listening to what another has to say."

- BRYANT H. MCGILL

My days are filled with many messages about the power of words. Words can change so many things. Even a single word can bring a whole new understanding to something. For example, when I say the word "magical," it tends to give you an uplifting feeling. When I utter the word "murder," it brings an entirely negative meaning.

One of my goals in my fifties is to listen more closely to words; to listen just for the sake of listening and not just to respond. Why? Because this will make me be more aware. Why is it important to be more aware? When the question was asked of several people at an energy workshop I recently attended, the consistent response was because it brings brightness and future possibilities.

I was with a group of ladies the other day and I just sat back and observed. It was very apparent that no one was listening to what anyone else was saying. They were listening in order to respond. They were literally waiting to respond instead of listening closely to what the other had to say.

Unfortunately, I think this has become a norm in our society.

Texting, unfortunately, has also become a norm in our lives. I can text someone all day, and they respond promptly. However, if I suddenly pick up the phone and actually call them in the midst of all that texting… guess what? They don't answer.

Instead of sitting in judgment of others, I decided it was time for me to be the change I wanted to see. I would be the one who listens carefully. The one who doesn't respond until I know someone has truly finished their thoughts. I was excited to see where this would lead. Would we have those uncomfortable bouts of silence that no one seems to like? Instead, I hoped that it would lead to someone being truly grateful that I actually took time out of my day to listen and value what they had to say.

After several weeks of paying attention, it seemed the more I paid attention, and didn't listen just to respond, the more others followed suit. I still have those in my life that talk over everyone, and listen to respond. In those cases, I just wait patiently until they are done before I speak. I can only hope that maybe one day, if they witness active listening enough, the practice will rub off on them. It's truly been refreshing to me when I am around folks who do take the time to really, really listen.

What a big shift for me. Pay attention, stop, breathe, and go into your next conversation in peace.

<u>now it's your turn</u>

What words mean different things to you? Are you on a path of becoming more aware? If so, why? Every word that comes out of your mouth has power attached to it. Where in your life can you make a choice to use different words? For example, perhaps you say, "I can't afford that." Try instead, "It's not in my budget right now." This puts another spin on your words and gives you different energy. I urge you to pay attention to what comes out of your mouth. Try it for a day!!

a soul's legacy of love
CHAPTER 12

"Everyone must leave something behind when he dies ... Something your hand touched some way so your soul has somewhere to go when you die ... It doesn't matter what you do, so long as you change something from the way it was before you touched it into something that's like you after you take your hands away."

- RAY BRADBURY

I woke up this morning to the news that *Furious 7*, the latest in the *Fast and Furious* movie franchise and the movie premiere I had the pleasure to attend, had topped $1.15 billion in ticket sales. During the time of its release, it held the #1 spot at the box office for three weeks running and it became the seventh biggest earning movie of all time – an amazing feat that some are calling the legacy of Paul Walker.

My first for that day was to find my voice (something that has taken me a long time to do because of certain family dynamics) and go up against some folks who are stating that Paul Walker's legacy is that he left this world by having a billion dollar movie. I know it definitely is part of his legacy, but as I have stated previously, his legacy goes beyond so much more than that.

Over the weekend I had an awesome girl's day with a soul sister of mine. She excitedly asked me how my trip to L.A. was for the *Fast and Furious 7* premiere. Can I tell you how nice that was? Someone made a point to ask me about one of the highlights of my year. That meant a lot to me.

In my previous "circles" it was rare for someone to not only ask how I was doing, but to also encourage me to talk about my life. I've changed out these circles, and now I'm experiencing more love and compassion. However, when someone takes interest in me, it still feels foreign since it's a fairly new occurrence. Regardless, it's an amazing and uplifting experience.

Someone asked me to describe what it was like being at a movie premiere. This led me to write this chapter. The question brought me back to what I was feeling on that exact night. When I recalled standing amongst so many people from so many walks of life, I realized that what Paul Walker's legacy exemplified was all of us sitting in that theater on that warm April night.

On April 1st hundreds of people gathered to celebrate not only the release of his last film, but also to celebrate the person that Paul was. To be honest, before his passing, I had never seen any of his films or had been familiar with him as an actor. But having met some of the folks who were in his "circle," I now have a really good picture of what he truly must have been like.

For that one night, I felt like all was right with the world, because I felt such true and utter love as a result of Paul Walker's legacy being acknowledged. I felt and saw what his family meant to him and what he meant to them. That night his family was not just biological, but also *situational*. His friends and his fans all gathered together in one spot and focused their love on one thing – Paul. How cool that so much energy was so big in one place. I saw the effects of what everyone focusing love, instead of hate or anger, had on a crowd and on the world.

Getting back to that amazing billion-dollar box office mark, here are my thoughts. I think that for this small moment in time, people around the world clamored to get that same great feeling that I did that night in Hollywood. I'd see folks leave the movie theater (having seen it again another weekend) with looks of pure and utter love. Everyone left the theater in a peaceful, yet emotional state. Perhaps it gave them all the impetus to reach out and share their love with someone else. We never know when our time, or that of a loved one, will come to an end.

Paul, I'm certain your legacy reaches more than just the box office numbers. I truly believe that your legacy is one of joining the world together no matter what their race, ethnic, financial, gender or any other group may be. You have proven that we can all get along together as long as we throw in that component of love.

It would be so nice if the world could continuously have the feeling I had that night in Hollywood. If we all came together with love and peace instead of hate, segregation, and negativity, where would we all be?

P.S. Not to diminish other parts of Paul's legacy, please check out his great work with his charity Reach Out Worldwide (*www.roww.org*).

now it's your turn

Where in your "world" can you bring in a little more love? Where can you practice acceptance? Is there a situation in your life that could use a re-boot, say a kid on your block who is being bullied or being a bully? Can you step in and make some shifts there? Maybe it's an adult who is excluded from something, take the time to include them in an activity. There are lots of situations that we can make into a different ending. What do you want your legacy to be after you leave this world? Do you want folks to remember that you were that person who took the time to smile at your barista or the grocery store clerk? No matter someone's position in life, we are all here on Earth to do good and share in this thing called "life."

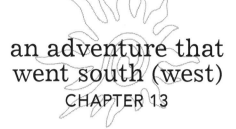

an adventure that
went south (west)
CHAPTER 13

"When adversity strikes, that's when you have to be the most calm. Take a step back, stay strong, stay grounded and press on."
   - LL Cool J

Mountain biking on Antelope Island, Utah; that sounded like a good item to check off my 50 for Fifty list. I had been to Antelope Island before but never mountain biked there. Sounds fun, right?

Let me give a little history on Antelope Island. The island has an area of 42 square miles, and is the largest of 10 islands that lie within the Great Salt Lake. Antelope Island has natural scenic beauty and holds populations of pronghorn and bighorn sheep, American bison, porcupine, badger, coyote, bobcat, and millions of waterfowl. The bison were introduced to the island in 1893, and since then the Antelope Island Bison Herd has proven to be a valuable genetic pool for bison breeding and conservation. The bison do well because much of the island is covered by dry, native grassland – according to Wikipedia. Lots more history there if you should desire to learn more.

So with bikes on car, helmets and water packed, I said, "Let's go!" It's about an hour and half drive from Park City. Before I knew it, my young son and I were there and ready for some adventure.

I suggested we check out the Visitor's Center, which is one of the first stops when you get off the causeway onto the Island. The center is a cement building perched on top of one of the highest points on the island. As I exited the car, I realized that there were swarms of gnats. Tiny, annoying bugs that fly right into your ears and nose. Okay, this should be interesting. Perhaps the plan might have to be modified.

Pushing forward onto the island, we decided that Buffalo Point would be a great trail to do. It's about a mile round trip and overlooks the Great

Salt Lake. I suggested we hike in a bit to see what the terrain looked like since I had my son with me. He is a great mountain biker on flat trails, but this one looked a little challenging.

Once we exited the car, it became very apparent that the gnat issue was not going to get better. Undaunted, I suggested that we abandon the bikes, but still hike to the topmost section of the hill. Bad idea! Anytime we stopped, we were absolutely swarmed. If ever a person were to go completely insane it might involve gnats. They were everywhere, moving with us as we ran faster and faster back towards the car. My son was screaming, I was screaming....

After finally getting back to the car, and getting whatever gnats were inside the car out, my kid declared that he never, ever wanted to come back to this island again. Can't say as I blame him.

As we started driving again, I realized we still had not seen any bison or antelope. One cannot come to the island and not see at least one of these animals. When I promised to not stop the car at all, my son agreed to continue down the road to find what wildlife we could see. We were rewarded with a herd of bison lounging on the beach, as well as antelope prancing through the tall grass.

Antelope Island is very scenic and beautiful. I am sure there are times of the year when the gnats don't swarm. I, for one, am not ready to venture back there again. However, the day was not lost. We soaked in some beautiful scenery, turned the mishap into a funny story, and ended up giggling the whole way home. My kid re-named it Gnatelope Island and kept saying we got "Gnatomic Bombed." It turned out to be a great bonding adventure for my son and me. We were met with adversity and turned it into a great day!

We began with high expectations of a beautiful mountain bike ride with amazing scenery. However, half way through we realized that there was something else in store for us. Instead of caving in and letting the circumstances change our attitudes and plans, we became very flexible and turned the day around with humor, laughter, and new (and even better) plans.

now it's your turn

Where can you use an attitude switch in your current life? Is there something that you could reframe from a negative situation into a positive? Stop for just a moment and think about this. Was there something that happened on the way to work, say in traffic? Did someone cut you off? How could you reframe that into a learning experience or better yet, something funny? It's all in your perspective. There have been days when I completely lost it because I was stuck in traffic and running late. Instead of grousing, however, I could have enjoyed sitting in my car listening to a great song on the radio. Who knows? By being late maybe I missed an accident that was the cause of the traffic. Count your blessings instead of cursing your stress!!

love and acceptance
CHAPTER 14

"And acceptance is the answer to all my problems today. When I am disturbed, it is because I find some person, place, thing or situation – some fact of my life – unacceptable to me, and I can find no serenity until I accept that person, place, thing or situation as being exactly the way it is supposed to be at this moment."

- UNKNOWN

I was lying in bed this particular Monday morning and had a wave of sadness wash over me. I realized that I did not have some sort of fun adventure planned for this week. It was going to be a week full of work, spring cleaning, and being the Mom Taxi that is a fact of my life.

However, as I was out on my morning walk, I had the clear realization that life's adventures and new things (*Aha!* moments) are not always just about fun, travel, and the next thrilling adventure. They also come in the form of a life lesson that sets you up for future greatness.

My husband joined me this time on my morning walk. We reminisced about the last 15 years and all the ups and downs we have had. We are currently in a pattern in our relationship in which we are working on ourselves. We have realized that in order to move forward in a positive and loving way, it was time to step back and take care of ourselves. This has come in the form of therapy, energy work, yoga, mediation, life coaching, and several other modalities. It's been a slow process, but one that seems to be moving in a forward and positive direction.

What brought up the *Aha!* moment during our walk was our discussion about a family member with whom we were both frustrated. We know deep in our hearts that this person's indecisions and fear hold him back from living his true potential. It's been a source of our frustration for years.

However, that day I had a moment, for the first time ever, when I stopped and said, "I've learned the difference between what I can and cannot control." It's taken me years of self-work to come to this, yet this family member is nowhere near the same revelation. He has made the conscious choice to stay stuck in old beliefs and limiting patterns.

Then I suddenly had another realization. "Why do we spend so much energy worrying about this person?" I asked my husband. "When we could take that energy and put it toward our own journeys."

It's super easy to direct your attention to someone else so you don't have to take care of your own issues. For example, looking back over my life, I realize I'd repeatedly advance a few steps forward in my own self-improvement, but then when the going got tough I'd revert back to my old pattern of "worrying about and trying to fix" someone else. How convenient! This takes the focus off me (and my challenges) and makes me think I'm using my restorative energies for a valid, *even better* reason!

That day walking with my husband was a great first for me. I saw that it is time to let this family member live his own life, so that I could focus more intently on my own. He is on his own path. I just have to accept and love him as he navigates it.

now it's your turn

What *Aha!* moments have you come up with in your own life? Was there a realization that hit you because you have been doing something for so long (to the point of exhaustion), but with no results? What aspect of your life could you modify to yield great results?

Like my realization with a family member, maybe there is someone in your close circle who needs love and understanding instead of changing or fixing. I'm a recovering "fixer" of people. My intentions are always good. I just want to help, but instead I end up wearing myself out focusing on people who don't want to be "fixed" in the first place. You can give folks tools they need to navigate their own life's journey, but then you have to detach and let them experience their own story. ***Stay in your own lane!!!***

a mother's day
spent in a new way!
CHAPTER 15

"Oh my God, my mother was right about everything!"
- *P.A. WALKER*

This new adventure had me on the road to Moab, Utah, a beautiful part of Southern Utah that encompasses several famous National Parks, including Arches and Canyonlands. The first in this adventure came about when my son and I decided to "glamp" at Moab Under Canvas (*www.moabundercanvas.com*).

What is glamping you ask?

It is a new word for a new kind of travel. When you glamp, there's no need to pitch a tent or bring a sleeping bag. These items are provided for you when you sleep in a yurt, airstream, villa, or in our case, a spacious canvas tent. I love to sleep outdoors, but sometimes you just don't have the time or energy to drag along your own equipment. When you glamp all is provided for you. Fantastic!

When we arrived at Moab Under Canvas, Ben, our park administrator, warmly greeted us at the reception tent. Ben went out of his way to make sure we were properly settled in our tent and had everything we needed. He helped with our duffel bags, pointed out a lot of the area information, and even suggested we order our breakfast for the next morning so we didn't have to drive down into Moab (about 10 miles away) after we got up. Ben also gave us some great tips for hiking and made sure we knew that he was available if anything should arise.

After settling in, we headed to Arches National Park. I have hiked there before, however, every time I go into Arches, I feel like it's my first experience. The red rocks look different every time. Around each bend of the road another stunning vista appears. It truly takes my breath away. The hike of the day was into an area called North and South Window. It's an easy hike to do, especially if you bring along the young ones. There are lots of fun rocks to climb up and over, and it's not too long of hike so (usually) there are no complaints.

After hiking all day and then enjoying dinner in downtown Moab, we headed back to our campsite. The weather this particular weekend was a bit iffy. The clouds kept rolling in and rain threatened. Rumor has it that the night before we arrived, a spectacular lighting show and heavy rain had hit the area. That would have been amazing to see from our campground. The scenery just from our tent was one that changed on a minute-by-minute basis. You could see the edge of Arches from the campground. As the sun was setting, the rocks kept changing colors – truly a phenomenal sight to see.

The next morning, which happened to be Mother's Day, I was greeted by an astonishing vision at sunrise. I hiked down to the reception tent to get a warm cup of tea (by the way, that tent always overflows with coffee, tea, hot chocolate, and great conversation with whomever happens to be at the front desk). It had rained pretty heavily the night before, which made for some wonderful sleeping. The storm moved, but not far enough to be completely done with us. As I exited the reception tent, I saw not one, but two full rainbows light up the sky.

It was one of the best Mother's Day presents I have ever received. My son even told me that he had ordered those rainbows special just for me.

We had originally planned to get up early and do a two-to-three-hour round trip hike to Delicate Arch Trail in Arches. However, since we woke to a gray, cold day, we snuggled in our extremely warm and comfortable beds and fell back asleep for a few more hours.

We ended the weekend by doing the Lower Delicate Arch Overlook Trail. This is literally a 100-yard trail that leaves right from the parking lot. You are treated to a great view of Delicate Arch, but not as up close and personal as the other hike. Next time, we will do the longer hike, for sure.

Moab is one of those places where the weather can turn on a dime; one minute sunny and the next raining with thunderstorms. We waited a bit, but alas, the weather did not break. It was time to head back to Park City and do laundry. How did we mess up our tent so much in just one weekend?

I am truly grateful to Ben and the rest of the staff at Moab Under Canvas for such a fun, memorable weekend. The company has other locations in Yellowstone and Glacier National Parks. Hmmm, which one to try next?

now it's your turn

Where have you had a new experience that opened up your life? Was it traveling somewhere you've never been? Was it ordering a new dish at a restaurant? Think of something original you can try this month. If we keep trying new things on this path called life, we keep our brains activated and don't become stagnant.

As we get older, it sometimes becomes scarier to try new things. We think, "Oh, I'm too old" or "I could never do that." Take away that line of thinking. It's never too late. You always have time, if you make time. If there's something you want to try, DO IT! Let this be that moment in which you say, "I can do this."

Enjoy, breathe it in, and post those pictures!

it's as if someone turned the light on
CHAPTER 16

"Faith is taking the first step even when you can't see the whole staircase."

– Martin Luther King, Jr.

I woke up that morning to the news that yet another earthquake hit Nepal. This time the 7.3 temblor was 42 miles from Namche Bazaar, close to Mt. Everest. I realized with a start that this is the area in which my niece's friend, Katie, had been trekking. I had a Facebook message from Katie not two days ago that she was fine and was staying there until she was scheduled to go to Khatmandu in two weeks. My heart sank when I realized that today she might not be so safe. I immediately took to social media to see if I could find an answer. It came via text message an hour or so later that Katie was indeed safe for now.

My 50 for Fifty first in all of this is that I truly realized *for the first time*, how quickly a life can be taken. In the blink of an eye an earthquake could hit and take dozens of lives. It never hit that close to home until I knew my niece's friend, Katie, was right in the heart of life-threatening peril.

With this new mindset, I proceeded to go about my day just a little differently. I had a new purpose. I realized that today could be my last day on earth. If so, did I want to spend it doing meaningless things? Did I want to spend it watching reality television, for example? (Not that I make a habit of that.)

No. I want to make every minute count.

Sitting at my desk that morning, I realized that I had an overwhelming urge to go and help *someone*. I didn't know what form this would take, but quickly realized that it would be one step in the right direction to send a donation to a *Go Fund Me* page that I have been reading about on Facebook.

My Reiki teacher, Carol Wilson, works tirelessly in Nepal helping people in need. Ironically, on Carol's most recent trip at that time, she landed in Khatmandu just five minutes before the big earthquake hit. She could have made the choice to turn around and go home, but instead she stayed to help out with relief efforts. I had been stalking her *Go Fund Me* page for a while, but now her fundraiser efforts were more important that ever.

I know it sounds trite to say life changed for me in that instance, but in some unexplainable way it had. Because of that earthquake, I made a deep decision to make changes and act on them immediately. It's selfish of me to not use this one beautiful life I have been given to forward my gifts to the world. What that looks like might not be so clear right now, but it is time to start moving in that direction and not be afraid to put my gifts out there. How many people has Carol directly affected by sharing her gifts with the world? It may be just 10… or thousands, but if she didn't have the courage to use her gifts in Nepal at that time, the world would be a different place for those affected by that devastating earthquake.

now it's your turn

How about just for today you take the time to see what changes you might need to instill in your life. Maybe you are in complete alignment with your purpose. If so, I commend you.

However, if you are not in alignment, I know the feeling. It's hard to put that first foot on unseen steps, but just imagine what we can do if we keep moving forward! What is one step that you could take right now to move your life forward? What are you holding yourself back from? Can you put aside your feelings of fear or hesitation and take one step towards the thing you fear the most?

Let me give you an example. A friend of mine has been meaning to learn Spanish for years now. She finally gathered the courage to spend a month in Spain, so she could immerse herself in school. As I write this, she is posting pictures on Facebook of all the fun she is having and all the neat people she is meeting. If she hadn't of taken that first step, she would have missed out on all of this.

You may not have the funds to go to Spain for a month, but guess what? I bet there is a free class at your local library. Whatever it is that challenges you to move forward, jump in and do it! That first step will most likely lead to new doors opening up!

signs from the universe
CHAPTER 17

"We are our choices."
- Jean-Paul Sartre

As I sat down this morning to write this chapter, it occurred to me that I had no clue what I was going to write about today. I just knew it would flow through me. This is a first of sorts. I liken it to just putting it out there. I choose to trust the Universe to take over the reins and give me a voice.

Today has been unique. I have had an outpouring of phone calls and messages from people that I haven't heard from in a long time. These are folks from which I have chosen to take a step back, because they didn't serve a positive purpose in my journey to move forward. They are not bad people, just not on the same path as me. But I questioned why suddenly they all reached out on the same day?

As the voice mails and emails appeared, I decided to sit with this and figure out what was going on. What is the pop quiz the Universe was putting to me this first day of the week?

I finally got it.

I realized after seeing several posts appear on Facebook, it was about going within. Why were these messages so bothersome to me? Why was it irritating that someone close to me was once again self-sabotaging himself? I pulled out the proverbial "mirror" and asked myself, why are these people triggering this worry in me?

And then it hit me.

I am irked because I made the conscious decision *to be irked*. I was spending my precious energy trying to figure out the behaviors of others… *yet again*. Do you know what this means? Time spent away from my dreams and visions. *Aha!* If I spend my valuable time worrying about others, then I don't have to go out into that uncomfortable world and deal with my own challenges.

When I realized all of this, I got excited. I have a choice. I *always* have a choice. I could continue going down that path of spending my time on comfortable, yet futile, efforts, or I could forge forward and do something that felt uncomfortable, yet was beneficial, to me.

I could *choose to* move one step closer to my dreams.

I could *choose to* do a huge thing today that makes a difference.

I could *choose to* do better today than I did yesterday.

Bottom line: It's all in my power. There are times when, of course, the behavior of others still affects me. It's only natural. But in those cases, all I can do is be there for others with compassion. I can ask, "What would playing bigger look like for you?"

now it's your turn

Is there a situation you keep re-visiting in order to get away from the bigger picture? If so, what will things be like in one year, five years, or ten years if you don't take action now? This is a pretty heavy topic, so I urge you to just relax into it. Pour a bottle of wine, put on your comfy jammies, light some candles, and sit with this question for a bit. I've taken a lot of time on this one, so don't worry that you might not have the answer today. It might not come next week, or even the month after. But just the fact that you have put it out into the Universe is a great start.

Hope you enjoy that wine!

my town through new eyes
CHAPTER 18

"My goal is to build a life I don't need a vacation from."
- R. HILL

A few months ago, I had the awesome opportunity to see my hometown through new eyes. My first for this chapter is that I decided to become a tourist in a town I have lived in for 15 years, but have started to take for granted and actually complain about (more on that later).

A friend of mine came to Park City for the very first time. She traveled to Utah from Northern California with her six-year-old son whom I had never met before. I loved this kid from the get-go. He is an old soul in a young person. What a beautiful outlook this kid has on life. He does things with gusto, with no complaints and definitely a lot of boy adrenaline. After just 10 minutes with him, I said to myself, why am I not living like this kid? Let's do this! Let's have a fun day.

We started out by having a late breakfast at Squatter's Brewery on the main drag in Park City (*www.squatters.com*). I have eaten there a lot, but never had their breakfast. I would say it was your normal fare – nothing amazing, but once you added a side of bacon, the rest just seemed to not matter.

Now that we were full, I suggested to my little friend and his mom that we head up to Utah Olympic Park. Utah Olympic Park is a fascinating venue at which several of the events were held during the 2002 Winter Olympics. There is an Olympic museum there, as well as plenty of fun activities in the park, including zip lining, bobsled rides, and a ropes adventure course (*utaholympiclegacy.org*).

My little friend, I'll call him D, is an avid Nascar fan. You could ask this kid about any driver and he could tell you their car number, stats, everything. To make the outing enticing to a six-year-old, I told him that they had bobsleds at the park where the drivers did upwards of 70+ miles per hour. My sidekick's eyes grew big when he asked if he could ride one. Alas, the track was closed and you have to be at least 18 to do this. But he wasn't disappointed, because we were able to do a simulated bobsled ride inside the museum. You sit in a chairlift chair and face a big screen that shows the bobsled track. You feel like you actually fly down the track, because the chair bumps and fake snow rains down upon you. What made it for me were the belly laughs coming out of D. He just had that pure, child-like giggle that took me out of the real world for a few hours and put me into the shoes of someone experiencing Park City for the first time ever. How cool was that?

Next up on the agenda was picking my own son up early from school. With D in hand, I went into my kid's classroom to surprise him and tell him that we were heading up to Park City's Historic Main Street and to Java Cow, the home of the world's best ice cream ever (*www.javacow.com*). We have been in here countless times, but never tire of the unique flavors. My favorite is Cherry Springer, a delicious blend of dark chocolate chips, vanilla ice cream and pieces of cherries. Divine!!

After walking around Main Street, we headed to Vinto's Pizzeria for some of their amazing limeade and to share a pizza. Vinto is our go-to pizzeria in the Main Street area. Being from New Jersey originally, I am a bit of a pizza snob. Vinto's is not East Coast quality pizza, but it certainly keeps me happy (*www.vinto.com*).

The day went by extremely fast. I realized at the end how much fun it was to look at my town with fresh eyes, and how much we enjoyed ourselves. As I stated before, I am getting a bit jaded about my hometown. It's all of a sudden become the place to move. It went from a quiet little ski resort to a big deal. The traffic is getting worse and the house prices are booming (okay, that last one is a good thing since I own a little piece of paradise).

But by spending the day as a tourist for a change, it gave me a new perspective. I realized that folks spend thousands of dollars to come to my town for a week's ski vacation or even just a long weekend. I live here. How lucky am I? I am now making a vow right now to cherish Park City each and every day.

<u>now it's your turn</u>

How long have you lived in your current hometown? Has it become just that, a town? I encourage you to take some time this week to look up somewhere in your town you haven't been to for awhile. Pretend you are on vacation in your town. Send yourself a postcard. It really invigorated me to re-appreciate where I have lived for the last 15 years. Don't take that town of yours for granted. There may be someone who is envious of you for where you live. But YOU get to live there. Appreciate it, enjoy it, and live it up.

dear wonder woman,
i am officially resigning
CHAPTER 19

"We change our behavior when the pain of staying the same becomes greater than the pain of changing. Consequences give us the pain that motivates us to change."

- HENRY CLOUD

The first for today is about finally finding the courage to set up some boundaries. It takes a lot of courage, strength and detachment to set up boundaries with loved ones and folks around you who suck your energy and life force right out of you.

This particular week I came upon quite a few folks who were emitting some intense energies. They were running programs of anger and frustration everywhere I went. I couldn't get away from it fast enough. I am a true believer of loving everyone the same, but sometimes people just really push the limits on that one. It was with this in mind, that I realized that it was time for me to find the strength to set boundaries.

This week I had two phone calls that really angered me. Why did they anger me? It was because I gave my precious time away to people that didn't respect or appreciate it. They had their own agenda, and did not come up for air long enough to ask me about what was going on with me. Again, I realized that this is my fault. I do not set boundaries. This has finally taken its toll. I am ready to take off my cape and forge ahead in a way that is healthy for me. This is the result of years of being a people pleaser and the go-to gal.

Why are we so afraid of saying no? Why are we so afraid to not set boundaries with those around us? Several reasons pop into my mind: What will people think of me? (Oh geez, there goes that line of thinking again.) We cannot say no or the old FOMO – Fear of Missing Out – kicks in.

It truly has been an empowering week for me. This boundary lesson got me thinking about other themes that run concurrent in my life. Why all of a sudden does this boundary thing bother me so much? Why do I all of a sudden have the strength to set them? I truly believe that because of the healing path I am on, I am acquiring increasingly more tools to help me handle these situations in a different manner than I ever have before.

Today I ran into two dear friends serendipitously. It couldn't have worked out any better even if I had planned it. These two lovely souls didn't know each other, but by the end of the two-hour chance meeting, they were chatting like old friends. I love that, I love to see that my tribe can expand beyond me and that I can connect like-minded folks. It also helped me to see that I was not the only one who had this boundary issue come up. My two friends and I had a lot in common that day, and it helped me cement that I was moving in the right direction.

I think we spend a lot of time blaming ourselves for past mistakes. Who doesn't? It's human nature. What I saw today made me realize that I sometimes slip back into my old way of thinking, but for the most part I'm correcting my course to get in alignment with my authentic self.

I love how the Universe helps us out.

now it's your turn

Where are you lacking in boundaries? What kind of stress are you putting on your body, mind, and spirit? Try instilling one new boundary today. Maybe you have been the one in the family who always cleans up the dishes. Instead try a new way and say, "Excuse me, I need some help here." I think you will find that those around you will be very open to your needs.

If you become happier, it will only benefit the others around you.

the ultimate road trip
(part one)
CHAPTER 20

"The world is a book and those who do not travel read only one page."

- *AUGUSTINE OF HIPPO*

The reason for taking a long journey began with the announcement of my nephew Dan's high school graduation near the majestic peak of Mt. Hood, Oregon. Dan is one of those kids that remained his solid sweet self since he was born. You really never knew that he hit teen-hood in the usual sense. He remained upbeat and happy. He truly embraces each day with vim and vigor.

When I got his invitation, it made me sit back and realize just how fast life goes by. Here was the cute baby I used to visit, who now had become a man and was going out into the world after completing the 12th grade. It was only fitting that I be there to join in the celebration.

After traveling by car from Park City, my son, his dad and I had our first stop of the night in Boise, Idaho. Boise is one of those cool towns that most people probably have not explored, but should definitely plan to do so one day. On this particular journey, we simply pulled into a hotel and spent the night. The real fun started the next morning when we hit I-84. All the way from home until the Oregon border, you can really crank it. The speed limit is 80 mph. But the minute you hit the Oregon border, you have to drop to 65. Seriously, how can you make any time at that speed? I pondered why this might be, but if you have ever driven this stretch of road, I really think it is so beautiful that they want you to slow down and enjoy the sights.

My first "first" of this trip was stopping in Pendleton, Oregon, for lunch at a cool place called the Prodigal Son (*prodigalsonbrewery.com*). I had the best salad ever: fresh goat cheese, toasted hazelnuts, sliced apples, and mixed greens with homemade cider vinaigrette. I also splurged on splitting an incredible cheeseburger with my son. This was by far one of the tastiest cheeseburgers I have ever consumed in my life. Every bite was a tasty morsel.

Pendleton is the ultimate western town. When you first pull into the downtown area, it feels like you become an extra in an old western film. There is even a giant cowboy boot on the sidewalk to advertise a very hip little store that sells all kinds of signs and household items. It's definitely worth a walk through. The name escapes me but it was right next door to the Prodigal Son.

As we wound our way up to our destination for the night, we spent many miles driving along the banks of the mighty Columbia River. What a beautiful sight. Since we do not have much water in Utah, it is always a treat for me to be around such big bodies of water. I just soak in the moisture.

When we rounded the bend on I-84 into Hood River, Oregon, we were greeted with our first glimpse of Mt. Hood. I have been visiting Mt. Hood for over twenty years, since I have family there. Every time I spot it for the first time on a trip, it never ceases to amaze me. Just look at the beauty and grandeur of this dormant volcano.

now it's your turn

Have you ever spontaneously taken a road trip? Loaded up the car and headed off to parts never traveled before? Have you always dreamed of doing this, but have been afraid to do so? Get out your map (or Map Quest these days) and circle places you have always wanted to go, but never made the time.

Then go do it.

Had I not gotten off the main highway in Pendleton, Oregon, I might never have had one of the best cheeseburgers of my life. If an exit looks like it has nothing on it, I still encourage you to get off and drive around. If you don't have a deadline or an itinerary, you will feel such freedom.

off to the beautiful emerald city i go!
CHAPTER 21

"In rivers, the water that you touch is the last of what has passed and the first of that which comes; so with present time."
- LEONARDO DA VINCI

Off to the beautiful city of Seattle I went! After spending five days in Oregon with family to celebrate my nephew's graduation, the road took us on our way to the beautiful city of Seattle. After we left our rental cabin in Oregon, we took the scenic route down through Hood River, Oregon.

Hood River is a quaint, little place on the banks of the Columbia River. As we wound our way through town, we came upon another idea for a first! Paddleboarding in the mighty Columbia River. No easy feat, as you watch the wind whipping down the Columbia River Gorge. Hood River is a mecca for windsurfers and kite boarders. Folks travel from all over the world to sport here. The beauty is jaw-dropping and the water looks inviting, but can be crazy dangerous with the currents and winds. We chose a mellow spot that appeared to be kind of its own little quiet enclave.

After getting in our swimsuits, we headed into the rental shop to get our paddleboards. This particular concession is right by the marina. The staff was really helpful and the equipment was perfect for our first foray into the river. As we dropped in at the mouth of the marina, it became very apparent that this was not your quiet, little tidal pool. Waves slapped at our boards as we struggled to navigate our way through the waters. After paddling for just a bit, the fun turned into surfing the waves onto the shore. Challenging, but a good time was had by all. It was a good workout, but now it was time to jump into the car. Our route took us over the bridge into White Salmon, Washington, and on down WA-14 towards I-5.

As the driver, I was the only one who did not get to partake in the heavy napping that was going on inside the car. The others in the car with me lost out as I got to see some incredible scenery along the banks of the river.

It's about an hour drive to I-5 when you come into Vancouver, Washington. We decided to stop and eat at one of my favorite places for lunch. Beaches Café (*www.beachesrestaurantandbar.com*) is a great spot where you can sit and look out into the river, enjoy the sunshine, as well as some great food. They are very kid-friendly at Beaches Café, and brought my son the usual placemat to color on, but it was the trip to the treasure chest at the cafe to retrieve a toy that brings a smile to his face.

The menu varies from burgers, shrimp, and all the way down the line to the wonderful beef teriyaki bowl that I decided to order. We had to, of course, finish up our meal with the delicious key lime pie that they have on their menu.

Back in the car we go and on I-5 north for about another two and a half hours. As we rounded the final bend into Seattle, that lovely skyline let us know our destination was near. It was a long day, but one filled with adventure. Knowing that I completed another first on my list made me realize how blessed I was to be living this adventure. The excitement of paddleboarding was amazing and having a great dinner at one of Seattle's cool restaurants, Rock Bottom (*www.rockbottom.com*), was the perfect end to a perfect day.

now it's your turn

Having the courage to jump into a raging river on a paddleboard was something that I wouldn't have thought I would do a year ago. Think back to a year ago and something you might not have had the courage to do. Take this time to applaud yourself for all that you have accomplished in the past year. Are you a different person than you were then? If not, think about taking one step in a new direction.

That's all it takes.

from the space needle to the gum wall – an adventurous day in seattle
CHAPTER 22

"I'd rather be hated for whom I am, than loved for who I am not."
- KURT COBAIN

We woke up to a warm and sunny Seattle day. That kind of sounds fake, doesn't it? Warm and sunny in Seattle! We mapped out our itinerary for the day, grabbed some breakfast and walked from our hotel to the check-in kiosk at the Space Needle. I highly recommend buying tickets online for the Space Needle, as the lines can get long, especially in the summer. Buying online allows you to bypass the ticket line and head right inside to show your bar code and ride the elevator all the way to the top of the 605-foot historic structure.

After growing up in New Jersey and spending a lot of time riding to the top of both the Empire State Building and the World Trade Center, the ride to the top of the Space Needle didn't seem all that long or impressive. However, when we stepped out of the elevator, the views were magnificent. All around you see water and snow-capped mountains. However, on that day, it wasn't particularly clear enough to see through the cloud layer and get a good view of Mt. Rainier. I had been to the Space Needle when I was about 18, but guess I never realized just how impressive Mt. Rainier really is.

I decided to do a little research and found out that this massive 14,000+ foot volcano is actually termed a dangerous super-volcano. Now doesn't that just make you feel comfortable? I guess the millions of Seattle/Tacoma residents just put that right out of their minds. To me, the beauty and recreational opportunities of living in Seattle far outweigh the risk of the volcano.

After the Space Needle, I was able to accomplish another first (hang on, as there were several on this particular day) – heading into the Chihuly Glass Gardens. Spectacular was the first word to pop into my mind when I saw this collection of glass works by Dale Chihuly. After spending a bit of time reading about this artist, I came to realize I have seen his work featured in both Salt Lake City and the ceiling inside the Bellagio Hotel in Las Vegas. Words cannot describe the beauty of this artist's work.

The second "first" for the day was heading down to Pike Place Market and into the Le Panier French Bakery. Wow, the food in there was delicious. I spent several years living in Belgium, blessed to be able to go to Paris quite a bit. Le Panier French Bakery was like stepping back in time to my years in Europe. The bread and macaroons were beyond divine. We had grabbed some cheese from the cheese factory next door, Beecher's (*www.beechershandmadecheese.com*), and combined with the bread and macaroons, a day spent in heaven was what we experienced.

When I travel outside of Utah, I am always amazed by how much better the food is for some reason. Is this due to the scenery? Better chefs? Fresher ingredients? I am just not sure. All I know is I was able to enjoy the best food I have had in a very long time.

No trip to Seattle would be complete without checking out the Gum Wall near the Pike Place Market. According to Wikipedia, The Market Theater Gum Wall is a local landmark in downtown Seattle, in Post Alley under Pike Place Market. Similar to Bubblegum Alley in San Luis Obispo, California, the Market Theater Gum Wall is a brick alleyway wall now covered in used chewing gum. Parts of the wall are covered several inches thick, 15 feet high for 50 feet.

now it's your turn

We've covered a lot of territory so far. Take some time right now to kick back, remember a journey you have been on, and visualize where you would like to go next! Take one step at a time, but keep moving forward.

kurt cobain, is that you?
CHAPTER 23

"Twenty years from now you will be more disappointed by the things you didn't do than by the ones you did do."
- MARK TWAIN

We ended our day in Seattle by dining at a wonderful restaurant called the Crow (*www.eatacrow.com*) with our good friends that moved to Seattle from Park City. Along with an impressive bar (whenever I leave Utah any bar is impressive, but this one really was!) the menu offered many delectable items. I decided to partake in the King Salmon since I was near the open waters and needed to fulfill my seafood cravings. It was delicious. Follow that up with an impressive dessert, a glass of Prosecco, all the walking we did, and this girl was more than ready for bed.

The next day saw us at the EMP Museum (*www.empmuseum.org*). Originally called the Experience Music Project and Science Fiction Museum and Hall of Fame, someone got the bright idea (which was a good one) to shorten the name to EMP Museum. According to their website, "EMP is a leading-edge nonprofit museum, dedicated to the ideas and risk-taking that fuel contemporary popular culture. With its roots in rock 'n' roll, EMP serves as a gateway museum, reaching multigenerational audiences through our collections, exhibitions, and educational programs, using interactive technologies to engage and empower visitors. At EMP, artists, audiences and ideas converge, bringing understanding, interpretation, and scholarship to the popular culture of our time."

That all sounds very cool, and the museum certainly lived up to its reputation and name.

We started our tour of the museum by visiting the Star Wars Costumes Exhibit. There were literally dozens of wonderful costumes, from Luke Skywalker to Chewbacca. My son is a huge fan and this exhibit really held his attention. The other exhibit that certainly caught his eye was the room with all the video games in it. It was like walking into a life-size Minecraft Game. I had to beg and plead to get him out of that room.

While my son was busy learning more than anyone ever needs to know about Minecraft, I wandered over to the hall that was filled with Nirvana goodies. This Seattle-based band was and still is one of my favorites. As I walked the halls and looked at guitars, sheet music, and cool photos from when the band was on tour, I could have sworn the ghost of Kurt Cobain was joining me on my tour. If you are a fan, do not miss this museum.

The EMP Museum has so much to offer every member of the family. We spent a lot of time in the Jam rooms. We were able to be "in-studio" while practicing our vocals, playing the drums, guitar and keyboards. Now mind you, I am so not ready to try out as a contestant on *The Voice*. However, it was a treat to watch Adam Levine and the rest of Maroon 5 in a music video projected on a movie theater-sized screen. Of course, we all had to dance and sing along. Don't worry, the rest of the crazy tourists were doing the same.

With our time in Seattle coming to a close, we bid farewell to the museum and it's helpful staff. One more stop in Cannon Beach, Oregon, and we were on our way back to Park City!

now it's your turn

All this travel has made me tired! I'm sure you might feel the same way. Relax, meditate and start working on that adventure list of yours! P.S. Jump on Pandora and listen to some Nirvana while you are doing this.

I'm sure Kurt would be impressed!

a new outlook
on an "old" body
CHAPTER 24

"Injury in general teaches you to appreciate every moment. I've had my share of injuries throughout my career. It's humbling. It gives you perspective. No matter how many times I've been hurt, I've learned from that injury, and come back even more humble."

- TROY POLAMALU

I broke a bone in my foot last year. How was that a first? Well, in my 50 years I can honestly say that I have never broken a bone before in my entire body. A great thing. This one was just a small one in my foot, but nevertheless it's been a great learning experience for me in several ways.

Let me explain.

I got up about 3:00 a.m. one day to answer the call of nature. As I walked into the bathroom I walked directly into a wall. I actually heard my bone crack. If you know anything about my town of Park City you will understand why when I went to urgent care, I hesitated to tell the front desk clerk how it happened. This is a small town, yet loaded with athletes of every kind. We have Olympians for skiing, snowboarding, and every type of winter sport you can imagine. We have triathletes, professional bike racers, both road and mountain. I hope you can see my dilemma. How can I go in there and say I walked into a wall? Really kind of boring if you ask me.

After the doctor confirmed that my foot was indeed broken, I went home with a walking cast and didn't realize that I was about to make a breakthrough in my thinking. What I mean by that is, this little old bone gave me a new outlook on life. I realized what a nuisance it was to walk around in this clunky cast, but I also realized how good I really have it. If I was complaining about a very small thing such as a walking cast, what would I be like if I were in a wheelchair? Or had to endure a broken back or neck? This little injury gave me an appreciation for the mobility of my body and the fact that it still worked just fine, albeit for the little inconvenience.

I had started a new fitness program probably six weeks before my injury. However, after this happened, I now, ironically, wake up each morning, put on my biking clothes and go for a road ride. It's as if I want to enjoy each and everything that I can do as an able-bodied person.

Fast forward a few weeks, and my foot is on the mend. Eventually I decided it was time to jump back into the yoga arena. I cannot tell you how wonderful it felt to be back in the saddle after several long weeks of not being able to do this. I was not 100 percent yet but I was getting there.

I am happy, yes happy, that I had this injury. As stated before, I was able to gain a new appreciation and a new focus in life.

Use it or you could perhaps lose it.

now it's your turn

Where could you gain a new perspective on something in your life? What could you show appreciation for that you previously thought was a nuisance? Take some time now to look around and see something you might not appreciate everyday. Is it a neighbor who says hello as you leave for work? Is it the kid down the street who offers to mow your lawn? Maybe it's time for you to do something different that others would appreciate.

Write down one or two things you are grateful for. If they are something you know someone else doesn't have, maybe you can offer that to them. By giving, rather than getting, you can open up the flow of energy into your own life!

a love affair with
capital reef national park
CHAPTER 25

"One cannot think well, love well, sleep well, if one has not dined well."

-VIRGINIA WOOLF, A ROOM OF ONE'S OWN

I cannot believe that I have never ventured south in Utah to the incredible area of Capitol Reef National Park. In my quest for doing new things this year, I added a trip to this beautiful area on to my list. I am so glad that I did. Capitol Reef certainly delivered in the *Beauty and Natural Surroundings* department. It's hard to put into words the beautiful scenery. How does one describe an area of the country that God spent extra time on?

Driving into Capitol Reef (which is about 3.5 hours from Park City, by the way) was the beginning of the scenery slide show. Beautiful red rocks were at every turn in the road. This particular National Park is one of the least visited in the country. I am not sure why, perhaps because of its close proximity to the "bigger" parks such as Bryce Canyon and Zion. However, it would be a shame for folks to miss this park. It's an area that is so different from any other. The geography and rock formations will blow you away.

Since my friend Sharon and I arrived in the afternoon, we decided that the first day in the park would be more of a driving tour. The Visitor Center is a great starting point to determine the direction and activity from which you want to embark. We decided we would take the scenic drive. This drive is approximately 20 miles round trip. Stay on it until the end, as the final leg offers, by far, the best scenery of all. You may see some signs along the way that deter you, but all you have to do is look up into nature. If the skies are clear, proceed in a straight line.

Around every bend in the road we elicited a surprised *ooh* and *ahh*. It was amazing to see so much nature and variations all tucked into one park. We wrapped up our day by checking into the Capital Reef Resort (*www.capitolreefresort.com*). Overlooking the red cliffs and one mile from Capitol

Reef National Park, this casual resort is three miles from the quaint town of Torrey. The rooms are comfortable, spacious and the resort itself has an inviting hot tub, which is quite the treat after hiking in the red rocks all day.

After unpacking our bags, we headed into the town of Torrey to check out a great restaurant for dinner called Cafe Diablo (*www.cafediablo.net*). This little gem is completely unexpected when you look at what surrounds it. It's got fanastic gourmet food, everything from Rattlesnake Cakes to Pumpkin Seed Trout. Every bite of my Watermelon and Feta Salad from start to finish was scrumptious. This was followed by my main course of Pomegranate Ribs and Butternut Squash Raviolis, which were the special that day. Each bite embedded such fond memories in my taste buds that I still cherish to this day. In fact, writing about it is making me want to jump in the car and head back down right now!

now it's your turn

Travel is a wonderful way to see both the world and your "world." I had never been to Capital Reef, yet it was only 3.5 hours away from my hometown. Take a map of your state and pick out somewhere close by that you have been saying you wanted to go to for years. It's time to make that commitment and go. Case in point, I grew up thirty minutes from Manhattan, yet ask me how many times I actually went into Manhattan? I, to this day, regret not going there a lot. I think of all the things that I missed out by not visiting it while New York was right in my backyard. Don't make that same mistake I did.

a beautiful beginning
to an adventurous day
CHAPTER 26

"Nature does not hurry, yet everything is accomplished."
- *Lao Tzu*

Day two in Capital Reef National Park brought about an invigorating hike early in the morning on the Chimney Rock Trail. This trail is challenging at the beginning because of the initial climb, but stick with it because you end up on top of the world. After hiking in washes with loose, sandy soil on miles and miles of rock, I was thrilled to note that the surface of this trail is hard-packed dirt. Much easier to walk on. In my opinion, Chimney Rock itself is not the most spectacular feature of this hike. You can see it from the road. Once on the trail, however, if you bear to the right, instead of first heading to Spring Canyon, the trail takes you higher than Chimney Rock and you literally have a birds-eye view of the park.

Continue on and you loop around and drop down into the canyon with its spectacular cliffs and vistas. Breathtaking. Don't let the steep beginning hold you back. Stop. Catch your breath. Look around. Then forge ahead. You'll be so glad you did.

Once we finished up the Chimney Rock Trail, it was time to start heading north back towards Park City. However, on the way we had two great discoveries. The first one was just in time for lunch. We came upon Duke's Slick Rock Grill (*www.dukesslickrock.com*) in Hanksville, Utah.

Let me explain what Hanksville is all about.

If you blink once you will find yourself on the other end of town. We gathered up our courage and headed into Duke's, which had probably 20 motorcycles parked out front. Now I am not opposed to motorcycles, but doesn't that just conjure up a vision in your head of entering a dark bar and every head turns and looks at you when you walk in? This restaurant was a big surprise. It pays homage to John Wayne, AKA The Duke. There

73

are cardboard cutouts of him everywhere. The best part of this restaurant, though, is it's cheeseburgers. Yes, cheeseburgers. They tasted like they were straight from farm to table. The Conqueror is a half-pound of seriously tasty, pure ground beef patty with cheddar cheese, served on a toasted bun with lettuce, tomato, onion, and pickle. It did not disappoint.

Along with the great food was the great staff. They really were attentive and friendly.

Once we filled our tummies again (do you notice a theme here?), we stopped in Goblin Valley State Park. Goblin Valley is out in the middle of nowhere just south of I-70 near Green River, Utah. What a cool, funky little place complete with hiking trails and a campground. It's really hard to describe just what this place looks like but for lack of better words, you feel like you are on Mars surrounded by giant aliens. It was a blast hiking all around the rock formations, playing hide and seek. One thing is for sure, I completely have to come back and camp here on Halloween. Just the name itself promises a good time during that season.

now it's your turn

Where in your life can you act like a kid again? Is it getting down on the floor with small ones and playing? Is it going bowling with a bunch of adults and laughing? Think about what a gift it would be to let go of life's responsibilities, even for a few hours. It will give you the presence of mind to just breathe, re-set and remember where we all came from.

five days in my happy spot
CHAPTER 27

"Traveling – it leaves you speechless, then turns you into a storyteller."

> - IBN BATTUTA

This past summer brought me to one of my most favorite spots on earth, the beautiful town of Santa Barbara. Although I had been there several times, on this trip I vowed to include several firsts. I was given the rare opportunity to travel by myself for five days as the rest of the family headed to Michigan to attend a family event. I looked at this as an opportunity to refresh and get to know myself just a bit better. I had no one to answer to and nowhere to be at any particular moment. I decided to see what the five days would bring me.

I stayed at a wonderful vacation rental that was just steps from the ocean. I was able to walk up and down 241 stairs in order to watch the beautiful sunset every night. My trip up and down the Mesa Lane Steps to get to the beach gave me the great idea to set a goal for myself of being able to run up the stairs without stopping by the last day of my trip. I was able to walk up without stopping, but because of my sore calf muscles, the running was just not going to happen. It was really encouraging, however, to see other folks run up and down several times with no problem. Quite impressive!

My days in Santa Barbara were filled with contentment. I was able to pick and choose what I wanted to do each day. The first full morning brought me to the Mission Santa Barbara (*www.santabarbaramission.org*). This was my first "first" of the trip. Founded by the Franciscan Friar Fr. Fermín de Lasuén, OFM on the Feast of St. Barbara, December 4th, 1786, Old Mission Santa Barbara, also known as the Queen of the Missions, has a history unlike any other landmark. It's got a rich and diverse setting, with beautiful gardens and surroundings. It takes just about an hour to wander through the buildings, so it's a good place to visit before heading to the wonderful beaches in and around Santa Barbara.

Before basking all afternoon on the beach, I had a scrumptious lunch at the Shoreline Beach Cafe (*www.shorelinebeachcafe.com*). Located directly on the sands of Leadbetter Beach, this wonderful restaurant uses fresh, healthy ingredients (produce, seafood, great wines), locally grown, harvested, and produced whenever possible. Their great wines, in particular, come from Santa Barbara County Vintners. Plus, the view is incredible, so it's not difficult to sit there for hours just gazing at the ocean.

Following up my lazy afternoon with a stroll down State Street, I was able to check out all the great shops along the way. Santa Barbara doesn't lack for amazing things to do.

I could get used to this!

now it's your turn

Can you carve out a little time for yourself that doesn't have an agenda attached? It doesn't have to be a five-day vacation. It could be as easy as shutting your bedroom door and taking a nap. It could be 20 minutes sitting in a bathtub or taking a solitary hike in the woods. By letting go of an agenda, you focus on yourself and your thoughts. If out in nature, you can take some time to connect with your soul.

Unstructured time ... it's the best

dining al fresco
CHAPTER 28

"We travel not to escape life, but for life not to escape us."
- ANONYMOUS

Santa Barbara always provides me with a few days away from reality. It truly is one of my happy spots. The ocean, scenery, people, and food make for a peaceful retreat.

As my adventure continued, I ventured out to try some new restaurants. One of the favorites of the trip was a place called Dargan's Irish Pub on State Street (*www.darganssb.com*). When I am able to sit outside to eat, it already adds points to a restaurant. This pub delivered in terms of both food and wait staff. A young Irish lad, who was in the States for the summer to work, pleasantly waited on me. He said he was excited to be going home because California was just too much for him. He provided great service and wonderful stories on top of that. Add my yummy guacamole, chips, and quesadilla entrée, and the night was a huge success.

While on my quest for full relaxation, I came upon the Float Luxury Spa (*www.floatluxuryspa.com*). Set in a small house on one of the side streets of downtown, this spa couldn't have been more tranquil. I opted for the Salt Scrub followed up by a hot stone massage. This is a life I could get used to. The staff was great, the facilities very clean, and the services divine. I will definitely be going back for more.

After all of this luxury, I headed to The Natural Cafe on State Street for a healthy meal. Since I was feeling very organic after all my treatments, I wanted to keep that clean feeling going. This tasty little restaurant provided just that very thing. It is an order-at-the-counter establishment, but then they bring your meal to your table. This place had it all; healthy food, drinks, and again, my favorite, outdoor dining. I really love to dine *al fresco*. Santa Barbara is the place just for that.

Too soon it was time for me to jet back to Utah. I absolutely love where I live. I always remind myself that people pay thousands of dollars to come to Park City to vacation. However, when I have a chance to be by the ocean, my soul is just re-nourished and I feel grounded. It always hits me hard when I drive back to my house at 7,000 feet. My dream is to some day live near the beach!

Baby steps....

now it's your turn

Have you ever dined solo? Or even better taken a trip by yourself? Some might be fearful of walking into a restaurant and asking for a table for one. I can remember just starting to do this when I traveled for business. I always felt the need to explain that I was traveling for business, because I thought the host/hostess might look down on me for being alone.

This was totally in my head.

As I perfected the art of dining alone, I opened myself up to having fun with it. There were nights when the whole wait staff would drop by my table to chat with me. Other times I brought a great book and just sat there with dinner, a glass of wine, and a good novel. It became very doable as the months went on.

When I started to travel by myself for work, it felt very natural. I looked forward to those nights in the hotel where I could take a bath, order room service, and watch whatever movie I wanted with no input from anyone.

If you have a house full of people, consider going to the local Hilton and staying by yourself for one night. You can't even begin to know how refreshed you will be after having only yourself to answer to.

a canvas of my experiences
CHAPTER 29

"Travel makes one modest. You see what a tiny place you occupy in the world."

- *GUSTAVE FLAUBERT*

I accomplished my fortieth 50 for Fifty "first" about three quarters of the way through my year of adventure. I have been talking about this one for YEARS. It finally took me turning the big 5-0 to act on it. My first tattoo, loud and clear on my forearm, is now a reality. Getting it has reinforced how proud I am of myself for making the plan to do this list, and completing it.

I made an appointment almost five months prior to the big day with a young man name Ryan at Oni Tattoo in Salt Lake City. He came highly recommended by a friend of mine who is very well-inked. I saw Ryan's work and immediately put down my deposit and waited out my five months. Not once did I waver from doing this. In fact, I was so excited that when it was time for my appointment I was 100% sure of walking in the front door of that tattoo parlor and getting my ink.

I had been grappling with several design ideas, but the theme seemed to be the same throughout: a sunburst. It was perhaps a week or so before my appointment when I was going through some old belongings, and an artistic tile I had bought in Sedona suddenly resurfaced. The design on the tile caught my eye and I said to myself, "This is it." I carried the tile around in my purse all week and every time I glanced at it, it became clearer. This was my tattoo. Never once did I imagine that one day it would become the design used in this book!

The process was a whole lot easier than I thought it would be. It took literally all of about 45 minutes. I had it in my mind that I would be there for hours, but once Ryan sketched the initial design, we made one revision and off to the table I went. Ryan had a great tableside manner that really put me at ease.

When he was done, he joked that I was officially on the dark side and now I would no longer be able to get a job! We laughed and immediately started talking about how long it would be before I came back in for my next. I am still considering whether or not to get some color on this one, a nice shade of purple might be the answer. This was reinforced as I was driving back up into the mountains from Salt Lake when I was greeted with an vibrant rainbow.

Getting a tattoo at my age was a bit unnerving, but it helped when I asked the young man at the front desk if I was the oldest person he'd ever seen come in and get their first tattoo. He smiled, and said, "No, ma'am. In fact, last week we had a 70-year-old lady come in for her first."

That made me feel great! Thanks dude!

When I got home that night, I showed my tattoo to my kid. He shrugged, said that's cool and off he went. I realized later that young people in his generation are probably so used to seeing tattoos that it didn't even make him blink. Let's hope that he waits until he is 50 for his first. If not, I will embrace his right to own his own body, as having this tattoo makes me feel that I own mine.

now it's your turn

What is something that you have been thinking about doing for a long, long time? In the case of my tattoo, I have literally thought about getting one for over 20 years. Is there something on your "list" that's been there for a long time? Something that you keep saying, "Some day I'll do that"?

Well, guess what? It's time!

Make a list of things that you have been putting off for the usual reasons of *I have no time, I have no money, I have no right*, etc. Take whichever item on your list feels the most compelling, rewarding, satisfying, and then get her done!!!!

Afterward, sit back and think about how cool or amazing that felt. Bring that feeling into your life more. Take on the other items on your list in the same way.

Once again... baby steps!

from chaos to calm!
CHAPTER 30

*"I am so busy doing nothing... that the idea of doing anything –
which as you know, always leads to something – cuts into the nothing
and then forces me to have to drop everything."*
– JERRY SEINFELD

Chaos. Yes, chaos. That word kept coming up for me. "I am so busy!" I notice people say this *a lot*.

"I am so busy I can't..."

On a daily basis people fill my inbox with things they were doing and wanted me to do. Finally, I stepped back and decided instead of getting frustrated or annoyed, I would detach and see what message I received. It took me all day to realize that I, too, used to be busy, busy, busy.

People tend to think that if their days are filled to the brim, they show the world how busy they are, which makes them look important. Or the very least, make them appear as if they have a very full life.

I know, because I was one of them.

When I worked in the corporate world, it would be a badge of honor to say, "Oh, I'm working late because I'm so busy."

One such busy day I decided to stop, sit with this idea of being busy, and see what came up. I have been spending a lot of time lately getting in touch with my feelings and figuring out what messages I am being lead to. I know, this might sound all woo-woo to some people, but I don't care. It makes me feel so much more grounded and present. Wasn't I trying to accomplish this for the longest time? Yes, my dear, I think that I have finally gotten the message. The first for this chapter is simply this: just be still. Be present.

I recently met with a relative who was telling me how much travel he and his spouse were doing. Caribbean Islands for the holidays, Mexico for a week, here and then there. The first question I asked him was, "Do you two ever sit still?"

He gave me the weirdest look.

"Do you ever just sit and be? What are you running from?" I have the nerve to say this because I was once a "runner," as well. Let's book an exotic vacation, be happy for a week, and then guess what? Your life at home is still the same. Do not get me wrong. I love travel. I crave travel. I also think that travel is one of the best things you can do for your life. See new things, experience new cultures, and sip margaritas at the beach. However, if you run from something, it helps to stay still long enough to address that *something*. Then you can go out on your adventures with a clear heart, clear mind, knowing that you will come home to that same feeling of clarity.

As I stepped onto my yoga mat that morning, I brought the word chaos with me. Does that sound as strange to you as it did to me? I decided to bring this word because it came up several times before I even got to the studio. Why, dear Universe, were you bringing me this word to meditate on today?

I came to the conclusion that it was officially time to calm down, be still, and sit in my own chaos to see where changes needed to be made. Another *Aha!* moment for my 50 for Fifty!

Please, take time to stop and smell the roses. Take time to spend quality time with your child before he is driving away to college. Take time to treasure every day. It's a gift that can be taken away at any given moment.

I love the way the Universe works. I love the way that it gently (sometimes more than gently) guides you to see what it is that it wants you to see. They say that the best coaches are the ones that give you the tools to help yourself.

Fortunately, the Universe has done just that for me.

now it's your turn

Where in your life you can skim down the chaos so you can better appreciate your life experiences? Let's all put down our phones, gaze out the window, and take a deep breath! Enjoy the gentle moment and bring that forward into our own lives.

conquering my goals
one fear at a time
CHAPTER 31

*"Fear keeps us focused on the past or worried about the future.
If we can acknowledge our fear, we can realize that right now we are
okay. Right now, today, we are still alive, and our bodies are working
marvelously. Our eyes can still see the beautiful sky. Our ears can still
hear the voices of our loved ones."*

- THICH NHAT HANH

Someone asked me the other day how I was doing on my 50 for Fifty list.

"Good question," I replied. It gave me pause, because I hadn't really been keeping track by the numbers. I just know that I have been having a great time in the process. This thought came about during a week in which I have been getting the huge message that life is not about the destination but about the journey itself. I need to look into this further.

I decided to go back in time on my blog and list the adventures I'd had. They included everything from getting a tattoo to conquering my fear of heights. That fear was basically conquered yet again with my latest first: Extreme tubing.

What is extreme tubing you ask?

Extreme tubing consists of taking a chair lift up to the top of one of the ski jumping hills located here in Park City. You climb out onto the top of the ski jump, jump in your tube and hang on for dear life. You have a helmet, which always tells me it's going to get crazy. It's just you, your tube, and 55+ mph of wind. Exhilarating, yet scary. Yet another way to feel so alive. I previously shared with you about snow tubing. Well, extreme tubing is a whole different genre of scary. It's the steepest, wildest ride you can imagine while in that darn inner tube.

Utah Olympic Park is right here in my backyard. It is a wondrous place that played a vital role in the 2002 Winter Olympics. It is still the training arena for aerial skiers, bobsledders, ski jumpers, and many a youngster who feels the need to be adventurous by engaging the park's alpine slides, rope courses, and the latest adrenaline addiction, extreme tubing.

It was threatening rain the day we decided to do this "first" (extreme tubing). Accompanied by two experienced 11-year-old-riders, I decided to conquer my fear. By the time we got to the top of the ski jumps (which is what you slide down at 55+ mph), it started to full-on rain. Great. That means the course would become even slicker.

They rushed people through the lines once the hail hit. It felt like having to evacuate a plane via the slide onto a runway. (I have never had to do this, and hope I never get the chance.) "Move, move, move" is all I heard. It was probably for the best because had I had to spend any time waiting on top of the hill, I most likely would have chickened out.

Into the tube I went. Onto the slick hill I went at top speed cackling manically the whole way down. I came in for a quick landing and realized that everything was intact. Now I had to figure out how to get my big derriere out of the tube itself. Once the mission was accomplished, we rushed into the restrooms to seek shelter from the bolts of lightening now streaking across the sky.

The day was a success.

It even included my son's friend calling his dad and starting the conversation with "Guess what, we're still alive." This is just what you want to hear as a parent. I love it!

Now that I am a certified adrenaline junkie, I look forward to the next chance to hurtle my body through time and space at 50+ miles per hour.

Whenever *that* will be.

now it's your turn

Where in your life can you just let go, and then GO fast? Why have you been holding yourself back? Try an extreme sport. Maybe your version of extreme sport differs from mine, or the guy down the block. Regardless, try a new sport you have never done before. Anything that lets you forget life for a bit and scream out loud is going to make you feel more alive.

sometimes it all just clicks
CHAPTER 32

"Just don't give up trying to do what you really want to do. Where there's love and inspiration, I don't think you can go wrong."
- ELLA FITZGERALD

Today was one of those days. What I mean by this is that it all just clicked and I became very clear on what I was put on earth to do. I am here to help people see their true selves. I am here to walk them to their greatest self by using several modalities.

I have been working on myself quite a bit the last couple of years. It's been a rough road, but would I have expected anything else on a healing journey? You may ask what prompted me to begin such a journey. It was a culmination of a few things. To sum it up in one sentence, I was getting uncomfortable in my dysfunction and was ready to have some different outcomes. I am here to tell you that it truly can be done. Don't get me wrong; I'm not done processing. It's a life-long journey, but one that I can now more easily traverse.

When one starts feeling like they're caught on the gerbil wheel, then it's no longer acceptable to continue that route. That's usually when we start to desire a different outcome. What is that old saying, "If you want something to change, you have to change something?" How simple but true. You simply have to change your reaction to something, someone, or some situation.

But how do some folks have the capacity to start their healing journey while others don't? I believe it has to do with mental attitude, capabilities, and quite simply wanting to get out of existing old stories. What story do you keep telling yourself that holds you back? What would your life look like without this story??

Ask yourself two simple questions:

1) How would my life look in a year if I don't change anything?

2) How could my life look different if I did make a change?

Which answer do you like better? Which one resonates in your body and soul? These questions have been very pivotal for me as I have embarked on my 50 for Fifty journey. Where do I want to be in a year? What do I want to be doing?

Listen, we have but one life to live. I'm sure you have heard that dozens of times, but what will it take for you to believe it, live it, and be proud of the legacy that you leave behind?

now it's your turn

Go back and re-read this chapter. I asked two simple questions above that I want you to really meditate on and journal about. 1) How would my life look in a year if I don't change anything? And 2) How could my life look different if I did make a change? Let me give you an example. I have an acquaintance who has complained about a guy she was dating now for a year. Same old story every time. I finally asked her those two questions above and it made a light go off for her. I asked her, do you really want to be sitting here at Starbucks in another year and have these same complaints? I told her that I didn't want to be sitting here hearing those same complaints. Time goes by way too quickly. Let's not waste another twelve months reacting the same way to something that hasn't changed. Let's change our reactions and see how that works instead!

time to let go of your old story!
CHAPTER 33

"Do the difficult things while they are easy and do the great things while they are small. A journey of a thousand miles must begin with a single step."

- Lao Tzu

How do you say goodbye? How do you say goodbye to one phase of your life and move into another? It's hard to let go of the past, but by doing so you say hello to the future. Letting go of your old stories makes room for the new. Everyone has stories that they hold onto for dear life. What does holding onto your story get you? It could be comfort, it could mean avoiding the unknown, and it could be fear – raw, deep, fear, plain and simple.

Moving from our old stories can be a mixture of things, but think about what your life will look like if you do move from your stories. It's the individual who chooses to move ahead that accomplishes the most life changes. Making these changes gives you the opportunity to step into your most amazing life ever.

now it's your turn

Sit down and imagine what your best self looks like. What are you wearing? What are you doing? Where are you working? Take time and see how this feels in your body. I bet it feels pretty good. If you are like me and can't get the thoughts out of your head long enough to visualize these pictures, then write it all down on paper. Do some journaling. Journaling is a great way for you to get these ideas out of your head and into your heart.

When you "see" your best self in your mind's eye, write down your willingness to do the work to *step into* your best self. What would this look like? Would it take hiring a coach? Exercising? Going to a therapist? Eating healthy? Moving away from family drama? In order to move into your best self, taking that first step is the most important move you can make.

Most people believe it's an all or nothing proposition to step into your best self. However, let me tell you that baby steps are the way to go. If you make a list of three things to accomplish in one day and you successfully do that, just think how you'll feel about your accomplishment. For example, if your goal is lose five pounds this month go out and walk for 30 minutes three times a week. If it's more than you are doing now, I bet that it will spur you on to move it up to 35-40 minutes three times next week. Little steps add up like you would not believe.

A lot of times that folks don't continue with their self-improvement is because they get frustrated. For example, they go all out and start a diet. Let's say they decide to eliminate sugar, fats and carbs all in the same week. What are the chances of success in that case? It will be pretty much next to nothing.

Instead start slow, eliminate one thing a day, or change up one thing a week, and look how far you will be in a month – most likely a lot better than when you started that month.

Making the decision to make some changes in your life is a brave move. Sometimes it starts as the result of no longer being comfortable in your dysfunction, or getting tired of living the same life. In any case, I applaud you if you were drawn to read this book. It means that there is some part of you that wants change!

I say go for it!

living my own reality show
CHAPTER 34

"So what do we do? Anything. Something. So long as we just don't sit there. If we screw it up, start over. Try something else. If we wait until we've satisfied all the uncertainties, it may be too late."

- LEE IACOCCA

Sometimes it's hard to think about life when it throws you a curveball. That's kind of what's happening to me right now. Life as I had imagined it would flow decided to show up and tell me that it has other plans for me. I could do one of two things:

Option A: Lay down on the couch, watch television and wait for the hardship to pass.

Option B: Stand up, look life in the face and say, "I've got this!"

I decided to go with Option B.

When faced with these two options, sometimes I have the urge to go with the first one. Boy, that couch looks soooo comfortable. I could click *On Demand* and cue up a reality show or an old movie, but instead I decide to live out my own reality show. I'm going to take those lemons and make lemonade.

Something became very apparent to me this weekend. I've decided it is time to move on. Move on from relationships, previous ways of life, and my life in general. How will this look? Not quite sure yet.

However, I actually put on Pandora and sang to myself in the shower. When I came out, I was excited about what the future holds. I can do anything I want! How's that for unnerving? I have the right to make my own choices, live my life on my terms and move forward to provide an exciting future for my child. I want to give him the best role model I am capable of.

We get plenty of opportunities in life to hit the reset button. Self-care is huge during these moments. Take time for meditation, salt baths, nature walks and self-love. Without our energy supply on its highest setting, we don't have the stamina to make it through those times when life throws you curveballs. Take a moment to collect your thoughts, look around and be grateful for what you already have. As long as there's a roof over your head, food to eat, and good friends, you can do anything!

now it's your turn

Where could you have made a different decision about something? What choices have you faced and how have you handled them? Everyday we are faced with the opportunity to change something for the better. Maybe we can decide to eat a salad instead of a Big Mac or change up that sugar-filled donut for a piece of fruit. As long as we continue on a healthy path and choose the option that gets us closer to our divine destiny, we will continue to shine in life! ***Make a different choice today...........***

family by a different name
CHAPTER 35

"But none of that really mattered. I had found my tribe. It felt like a family reunion for the family I'd never really known, a homecoming at the place where I was always meant to be but hadn't known how to find."

- DAVID LEVITHAN, HOLD ME CLOSER: THE TINY COOPER STORY

A visit from family is something to cherish.

Or is it?

This past week I had the pleasure of having my brother's ex-wife visit me here in Utah. In the 15 years that I have lived here, she's never made it here, until now. And now that she has, she is a fan of our beautiful state.

Her visit got me thinking about how my family life has evolved over the last 10 or so years. I am one of five siblings, the youngest. My siblings are spread out all over the United States from Oregon clear across to New Jersey and South Carolina. We also throw Arizona into the mix. There is a reason we all live in different states. In fact, there are several reasons. But that's the subject for another book.

What I started to think about while my ex-sister-in-law was here was how I define family *now*.

For starters, she is on paper my ex-sister-in-law, but in my heart and on the phone, for all intents and purposes, she is my sister. I have known her since I was 12. She could tell stories about me that even I don't remember. I appreciate her, I cherish her, and we had the best visit ever.

It got me laughing when I introduced her to folks. We look nothing alike, but I introduced her as my sister. You see, my biological sister is someone that I have nothing in common with except being born to the same parents. I haven't seen her in years, and I know for a fact that she probably gets her information about me by way of Facebook via my niece.

My niece rocks, she is an interesting young lady who appears to have more of my traits than my sister's. I pray that someday soon my niece moves west so I can get to know her all over again.

Family these days, according to most of my neighbors and friends, is a mix of biological and self-made. I love my Park City family (friends). They treat me with more respect than I get from most of my siblings. I cherish the time I spend with them and enjoy their company. I have more in common with the family I choose than I do with the family I was born into.

I once read a book called, "Why Do I Love These People" by Po Bronson. I highly recommend it. The subtitle is "Understanding, Surviving and Creating Your Own Family." It's like he wrote this book just for me. Now don't get me wrong, my family has its good traits. But I am the "different" one. If you are that one in your family, you know what I mean. I am the one seeking answers as to why we operate in certain ways. I ask the questions that nobody wants to talk about. You can imagine how well that goes over.

As I get up in years, I have come to realize that society imposes quite a few "rules" about how families should operate. I think Norman Rockwell's famous 1943 painting "Freedom from Want," the one of family dinner at Thanksgiving, probably did a number on a lot of us. Holidays are now defined by this painting. Honestly, how many times does real life look like this? I know for a fact, that it's been a very long time since mine has.

It's taken me awhile to come to the realization and knowledge that you pick your family for a reason. Some folks even say this happens prior to birth so that you can come into this life and learn certain lessons that hopefully correct certain things. I am a believer in this. There are days where I think, *What the hell am I supposed to learn from this?* It all gets back to the basic messages of unconditional love and letting folks navigate their own journeys. It takes patience, as well as giving up the need to be right. Just because I operate one way doesn't mean that I should expect anyone else to operate the same way.

There are days where I get sad because I don't have one of those families that pack up and meet all in one destination for a week of fun. In fact, a few years ago my sister tried to make that happen and 98 percent of us said *no, thank you.*

When I spoke with my visiting "sister" (i.e. ex-sister-in-law), I admitted that the next time I see my biological family all in one place it will be at someone's funeral. But at the same time, I also remember that I do have a "family" that I adore. I have assembled my own tribe, which includes my child, friends, and neighbors. We have similar interests and encourage each other to be our greatest selves.

I love, love, love this.

now it's your turn

What does your version of family look like? Do you have the gift of having a close-knit family? Or have you drawn together like-minded folks and formed your own tribe?

Either way, you have the support of other folks. If you are distanced from your family of origin and it upsets you, I urge you to look around to see who has your back. Is it a best friend who invites you to her house for holidays? Is it a co-worker who asks you how you are everyday? Family, these days, is comprised of more than just who you born and raised with. Family includes those folks that have embraced you in other ways.

Always remember you are not alone.

a journey completed
CHAPTER 36

"Because everyone has a natural yearning for completion, we are able to change and recreate ourselves endlessly."

- ILCHI LEE, THE CALL OF SEDONA: JOURNEY OF THE HEART

So here it is, the last post for my 50 for Fifty year long mission. I'm so blessed and amazed that I was able to accomplish all that I set out to do. When the time came to do my last 50 for Fifty "first" it all worked out so organically and flowed so nicely that I couldn't even fathom it.

Let me explain.

When I thought about what to do for my last "first" I somehow imagined something big (perhaps a trip or night out) with some of my closest lady friends. However, timing and school breaks had other plans for me. That weekend found me heading to Las Vegas and on to Southern California for my son's fall break from school. After a bit of pondering, I realized that since he had been on my first adventure, it was only fitting that he go on my last adventure, number 50!

Last year I had been too afraid to go on the world's largest Ferris Wheel, which just happens to be in Las Vegas. This year, I decided, what the heck? What a great way to end this grand adventure of mine.

If you have never been to this Ferris Wheel called the High Roller, it's a pretty big deal. The top of the High Roller is 550 feet up in the air. The views are amazing from start to finish. Once you board your *pod*, you continue moving for the full rotation of the Ferris Wheel. It moves so slowly that there is plenty of time to *ooh* and *ahh* over the Las Vegas Strip, the sunset, the mountains, and the desert beyond. We were able to see the sunset and even the dark skies of night. All in all, it takes about 30 minutes for your ride to be complete.

It was very fitting that this ride was fiftieth on list, being that it stopped at 550 feet up in the air. My chilled glass of champagne was very celebratory to mark this auspicious occasion.

This year has been a year of fun, new things marked off my bucket list and many *Aha!* moments that have propelled me into a new way of life.

How does it feel to complete what I set out to do? I can't even begin to describe the exhilarating sense of accomplishment. Finishing this list is huge for me. I am the queen of *start-something-and-then-not-finish-it-before-I-start-something-new*. As a result of my achievement, I feel empowered and excited to usher in my new decade. The feeling I had while I was 550 feet up in the air was one of complete jubilation. I did it! I really did it!

Thank you for coming along on this epic adventure with me. I'm not done with my escapades just yet. This list of fifty has inspired me to continue on with new ideas, trips, and better ways to operate my life.

Stay tuned …

anything you dream is possible!
EPILOGUE

"Don't you ever get the feeling that all your life is going by and you're not taking advantage of it? Do you realize you've lived nearly half the time you have to live already?"

- Ernest Hemingway, The Sun Also Rises

On Monday, February 1, 2016, James Twyman walked into ISIS controlled Syria to perform his peace concert. He had asked his tribe previously if everyone would say a prayer of peace at the exact same time throughout the world. I programmed that exact moment to pray into my phone, so I could be a part of the collective. As the time neared, I actually got chills and felt like there was a powerful energy building up. I wanted to tap into it and give my support.

This whole process got me thinking as to what makes up an individual such as James Twyman? Why is it that some people kick ass and do important things, while others believe just getting by is enough? It's an interesting thing to ponder. Why am I driven by a desire to look deep inside for answers, even though there are those out there who live a completely normal life staying home and just surviving?

The difference? I want to thrive.

I am realizing now that the James Twyman's of the world usually have been through some earth-shattering situation that turned their lives around in a minute. There are the cancer survivors who say, "Cancer is the best thing that ever happened to me." There are people who have lost loved ones and are well aware that life is just too darn short to waste a second of it.

I'm on *that* path.

Losing someone with whom I had a connection changed my life in just one day. The path that I'm on since his sudden death has been one that has not only awakened me, but also those around me.

Remember the story of Randy Pausch, the charismatic young college professor who chronicled his battle with pancreatic cancer in a remarkable speech widely known as the "Last Lecture?" If you have never read this book or seen his lecture, I highly recommend it.

Mr. Pausch points out a few important factors in this video, the most important being this: "Anything you dream is possible." He talks about how to live life as if you were dying because, well, he was dying. I watched this video and said to myself, "If this man is so inspirational and upbeat in his last few months, what could I do here on earth without being sick?"

Imagine the possibilities.

The lesson that has come through loud and clear for me over my 50 for Fifty year is that life is short. We are all going to die. No one gets out of here alive. With that in mind I decided it was time to take some action and live the best life that I can! What does that look like? It's a daily work-in-progress.

I have been given the gift of this realization by the folks I have lost way too soon. The best way that I can honor their memories is to live my life to the fullest. I know they are around me everyday. I feel them. I talk to them. Obviously they might not talk back, but I know in my heart that they are there to support me.

And always will be.

here's my 50 for Fifty list

1. Hiked the Stewart Falls Trail in Sundance, Utah, to conquer an old fear.

2. Got braces.

3. Sorted down my "stuff" in order to make the realization that I no longer needed my "stuff."

4. Overcame end-of-life fears through snow tubing at Solider Hollow in Midway, Utah.

5. Surrendered to the Universe and turning real with my writing.

6. Attended race car school at Exotics Racing in Las Vegas, Nevada (*www.exoticsracing.com*).

7. Re-worked my Circle of Influence.

8. Traveled and stayed in Kanab, Utah, for the first time ever.

9. Ate at the Heartline Café in Sedona, Arizona (*www.heartlinecafe.com*).

10. Hiked the Boynton Canyon Trail in Sedona, Arizona.

11. Ate at the Chocola Tree Restaurant in Sedona (*www.chocolatree.com*).

12. Experienced the Vermillion Cliffs in Southern Utah.

13. Attended the movie premier of *Furious 7* in Hollywood, California.

14. Listened more closely to people. I now listen not to respond but to really listen.

15. Found my voice for the first time.

16. Mountain biked on Antelope Island in Utah.

17. AHA Moment – Learned to stay in my own lane and let others be in charge of themselves.

18. Glamped in Moab, Utah (*www.moabundercanvas.com*).

19. AHA Moment – Strive to make everyday of my life juicy. Life is short.

20. AHA Moment – Go within – mirroring. Figured out why people are triggering me.

21. Saw my town through new eyes.

22. Found courage to set some boundaries.

23. Had lunch at the Prodigal Son in Pendleton, Oregon (*www.prodigalsonbrewery.com*).

24. Paddleboarded in the mighty Columbia River (Hood River, Oregon).

25. Had dinner at Seattle's cool restaurant – the Rock Bottom (*www.rockbottom.com*).

26. Visited Chihuly Glass Gardens in Seattle (*www.chihulygardenandglass.com*).

27. Visited Le Panier French Bakery – Pike's Place Market, Seattle (*www.lepanier.com*).

28. Experienced Beecher's Hand Made Cheese – Pike's Place Market, Seattle (*www.beechershandmadecheese.com*).

29. Ate at the Crow Restaurant in Seattle (*www.eatacrow.com*).

30. Visited the EMP Museum in Seattle (*www.empmuseum.org*).

31. AHA Moment – Breaking a bone gave me a new appreciation of nurturing my body.

32. Went to Capital Reef National Park, Utah.

33. Ate at Café Diablo (*www.cafediable.net*).

34. Hiked Chimney Rock Trail in Capital Reef National Park.

35. Ate at Duke's Slick Rock Grill in Hanksville, Utah (*www.dukesslickrock.com*).

36. Went to Goblin Valley State Park, Utah.

37. Traveled solo with a new perspective.

38. Ran up and down the Mesa Lane Steps in Santa Barbara, California.

39. Visited Mission Santa Barbara (*www.santabarbaramission.org*).

40. Visited Shoreline Café (*www.shorelinebeachcafe.com*).

41. Visited Dargan's Irish Pub, Santa Barbara (*www.darganssb.com*).

42. Visited Float Luxury Spa (*www.floatluxuryspa.com*).

43. Ate at Natural Café, Santa Barbara (*www.thenaturalcafe.com*).

44. Got my tattoo.

45. AHA Moment – Learned how to go from Chaos to Calm.

46. AHA Moment – Life is not about the destination, but the journey itself.

47. Went extreme tubing at Utah Olympic Park (*www.olyparks.com*).

48. Let go of my old story.

49. Found what makes my soul say yes!

50. Went on the High Roller ferris wheel in Las Vegas (*www.caesars.com/linq/high-roller*).

51. Bonus = Finished what I set out to do by blogging about this incredible journey!

anything you dream is possible!

now it's your turn

List Your 50!

1.

2.

3.

4.

5.

6.

7.

8.

9.

10.

11.

12.

13.

14.

15.

16.

17.

18.

19.

20.

21.

22.

23.

24.

25.

26.

27.

28.

29.

30.

31.

32.

33.

34.

35.

36.

37.

38.

39.

40.

41.

42.

43.

44.

45.

46.

47.

48.

49.

50.

acknowledgements

I have been guided and supported on this journey of writing a book by a beautiful group of people that helped me to see my future potential and were the main cheerleaders for this book.

First and foremost, Stacy Dymalski, without your guidance and coaching, this pile of papers would not have come to fruition. Your gifts are endless. Own them and know that you are making a huge difference in a lot of peoples' lives. For you aspiring authors out there, check out Stacy's wonderful programs at *www.thememoirmidwife.com*.

Michael H. Your precise words at our Epic event were what put me on track to get this book into the Universe. I so appreciate your talent, wise words and zest for life. The forward that you wrote for this book moved me to tears!

Becca M. I cannot even put into words what you mean to me. You've been the gas pedal in my race car, my transportation mode for staying in my own lane and moving my life forward. Please own what a rock star you are. Your comments to me about making my book title sassy were priceless – "You got a tattoo and are not teaching people how to crochet for Christ's sake!" was worth a ton of giggles plus a title shift.

Melinda Morris, you are my rock. Our talks at Hugo Coffee (*www.hugo.coffee*) were such a catalyst to bring this project to the finish line. Your sense of humor, beautiful Southern charm, and great energy helped keep me buoyed up to see this through to the end. I so look forward to reading your work of art.

Martha Markus, my Canadian lovely. Your intuition, sassiness, friendship and love were a major support for me. I can always count on being able to pick up the phone at any time of day and knowing your lovely voice was on the other end to either talk me off a cliff, give a great piece of advice or for simply a laugh to change the direction of the day. I truly appreciate every ounce of you.

Katie Mullaly, can we still have our lunches at the hospital café? I so enjoyed working with you on this journey. Your design skills are top notch (*www.facetedpress.com/book-layout*). Your talent as both a designer and an author is going to take you places that you will not even know exist yet!

Jennifer M. Lots of laughs over lunches. You have always encouraged me to finish my book! Your friendship means the world and I can't wait for our next round of lunches to discuss my sequel, "You Couldn't Make This Shit Up if you Tried!"

Sharon and Suzanne, your creative minds are what helped me to see the finish line on my book title. When one gets goose bumps, you know you are surrounded by great talent. You two ladies have that plus more. Lots of love to you both.

Stephanie B, Carina, and the rest of my lovely "tribe" (you know who you are!). Your encouraging words, energy healings, and just pure love supported me on this journey from the get-go. Your beliefs in my abilities are beyond priceless. Much love!

To my siblings, especially my brother John who was the catalyst for this process, although we are in five different states, each and every one of you has come from the same beginnings as I. Your paths have given me ample material to build my own life. You have also brought into my life numerous nieces and nephews who are the loves of my life. Who knew that a pack from Jersey could turn out so okay! XOXOX

Momma D and Auntie Syd, my beautiful souls who were lost too young to cancer. You were role models in helping me say yes to my soul. Your presence in my life was a priceless gift that came exactly when I needed it. I miss you each and every day but am comforted to know that your angel wings surround me.

To my son, Kyle, you are my inspiration and my greatest joy. Our dance parties, adventures, road trips, and giggle fests are what life is all about. You have the potential to be anything you want. You've asked me on several occasions what your "path" is in life. Be a kid right now, but know that since you are asking that question you are destined for great things.

To my partner in this thing called life, Tim, no matter where the wind blows us, I know that you have my back. Our commitment to co-parent our child in a happy, healthy manner is precious to me. You are working on your journey, while I am working on mine. I am excited to see where it takes us both.

Last, but certainly not least, to Paul W. Words cannot express to me how my life has changed since our paths have crossed. Your passing was tragic, but it was also a catalyst for my life to completely change. You were an actor and philanthropist, a dad, a brother and a son who made his mark in the world. You are there in spirit and synchronicity every step of the way and for this I am eternally grateful.

about the author

Trish Walker has been on a spiritual journey for three years during which time she became a Certified Reiki Master and Holistic Health Coach.

A Certified Life Cycle Celebrant™, Trish performs life union ceremonies for couples, and is the owner/operator of her business, Ceremonies With Spirit. Her popular blog *Fifty for a Year* (*www.50forayear.com*) and her family keep her grounded and remind her of what is important in life.

She lives in the beautiful mountain town of Park City, Utah, while not on the road during one of her many adventures.

For more about Trish and her continuing adventures visit *www.trishwalker.us.*

Made in the USA
San Bernardino, CA
08 October 2016